"AAPIs have a long and storied history in California politics and will continue to play an ever-important role in the future of the Golden State. Bill Wong's tremendous career within the cauldron of politics make his insider's view a must read."
— **Sara Sadhwani, PhD, Assistant Professor of Politics at Pomona College and California Citizens Redistricting Commissioner**

"I am absolutely excited that Bill Wong has authored an amazing book to inspire and empower the AAPI community, as well as every community that has suffered by bigotry, hatred, racism and division in this country and in this state. These writings chronicled by this great man will be transformative and empowering."
— **Mike Gipson, California Assembly Democratic Caucus Chair**

"I would recommend this book to anyone interested in California politics with an emphasis on Asian-American issues. Bill's book perfectly captures the significant successes and struggles that Asian-American Pacific Islanders have experienced over the past two decades."
— **Bryan Ha, California Faculty Association Director of Government Relations**

"Bill Wong converted his lived experiences into practical political change."
— **Richie Ross, Ross Communications**

"Bill Wong's book provides a profound analysis of ideological forces vying to define the future. His incredible anecdotes tell stories about political leaders facing systems that serve the few at the expense of the many and promote a new consciousness of what it means to be human on this planet run by political beliefs. This powerful book inspires and empowers actions that manifest an awakening to our collective political system and a reawakening of how we see the world. A must read for anyone who believes in the power of change, progress, and hope."
— **Phil Chen, California Assemblymember**

"Make no mistake about it, Bill Wong is committed, skilled, and wise. His insights are the products of broad and deep experiences combined with fundamental respect for others. His sense of solidarity makes for richer public discourse and more thoughtful civic engagement."
—**Mark Ridley-Thomas, former Los Angeles County Supervisor, California State Senator, and State Assemblymember**

"Bill commands respect and admiration for good reason. He was always the x-factor opponents feared and the secret weapon allies needed. In the years to come, the decade between 2012 and 2022 will come to be known as the Bill Wong era of politics."
— **Ian Calderon, former California Assembly Majority Leader**

Better to Win

Praise for *Better to Win*

"*Better to Win* is the best book I've ever read that deals with practical political and personal power—how to acquire it and more importantly, how to use and strengthen it. I believe the takeaways and lessons from this book can benefit everyone and anyone who's interested in making a difference in the political arena."
— Jadine Chin Nielsen, former Deputy Mayor of Los Angeles

"Bill is a selfless, fearless, and formidable operator working in the shadows for decades to politically empower Asian Americans. Much of our success today is owed to his efforts. AAPIs need this book, which will help immensely in our fight to increase our voice and our power."
—Judy Chu, U.S. Congresswoman and chairwoman of the Congressional Asian Pacific American Caucus

"Bill Wong, among the very best political strategists of our times, offers unique insights into one of the most significant groups of voters and provides fascinating behind the scenes details about campaigns and political battles he helped wage. Bill has written an essential guide to the politics of Asian American voters and provides wise lessons in leadership."
—Dan Morain, author and former Editorial Page Editor for
The Sacramento Bee

"I've always thought of Bill Wong as equal parts Machiavelli, Freud, Rasputin, and Kafka which was why I've always sought his counsel. If you're in a fight, he's who you want on your side when the odds and establishment are against you."
—Anthony Rendon, California Assembly Speaker

"Bill Wong is an exceptional and rare political 'operative'. He builds relationships and identifies leaders. He is a masterful tactician and understands and identifies the intersection between policy and politics. His book gives us a rare insight into how 'to get things done' in California's state capitol. The lessons from this book can, and should be, applied to all levels of government by community activists and aspiring politicians alike."
— Alberto Torrico, former California Assembly Majority Leader

"When everyone else is afraid to go to war, Bill Wong isn't. We need more fearless, tenacious, and selfless leaders like him."
— John Chiang, former California State Treasurer and State Controller

"Bill Wong gives voice to our struggles and our hopes. AAPI leaders have fought hard to gain a seat at the table, often opting to stand if none was offered. *Better to Win* reminds Asian Americans where we have been, how far we've come and how we got here, and sets the stage for an important truth—we are just getting started."
— Jill Tokuda, U.S. Congresswoman

"Bill Wong is the street smart, no-BS older cousin in politics we all wish we had. His understanding of power—the way it works, the glittering decoys that lead us away from it, and how to wield it with honor rather than glory—is piercing. His decades in the trenches, and the upper echelons, of Democratic politics are a treasure trove of knowledge for the AAPI community and for anyone serious about building lasting power for marginalized people."
— Sonia Chang-Diaz, former Massachusetts State Senator and gubernatorial candidate

"There is no one in the United States who is more experienced, savvy, and talented in terms of AAPI politics than Bill Wong. This book is a must-read for anyone seeking to understand the lay of the land in AAPI land."
— Garry South, Democratic Strategist and Commentator

"Bill is a transformative innovator and disruptor in California's high stakes political arena whose unconventional approach to leadership and strategy led to historic wins for Assembly Speaker Anthony Rendon and the Assembly Democrats. His commitment to helping others and elevating opportunities for all is what makes him so special."
— Tom McMahon, Partner at The NP Agency and former Executive Director of the Democratic National Committee

Better to Win

Win

Hardball Lessons in Leadership, Influence, & the Craft of Politics

Bill Wong

RONIN ROAD PRESS

Published by Ronin Road Press

To contact the author about speaking, consulting, or ordering books in bulk,
visit www.BettertoWin.com

ISBN (paperback): 979-8-9878036-0-8
ISBN (ebook): 979-8-9878036-1-5

Edited by David Aretha
Cover and Book Design by Christy Day, Constellation Book Services
Cover Photo Credit: Cristal Wallin
Author Photo Credit: Cristal Wallin

Printed in the United States of America

"If you succeed without suffering, it is because others have suffered before you. If you suffer without succeeding, it is so that others may succeed after you."
—Unknown

With greatest love, gratitude, and respect to my grandmother, grandfather, mother, and father for crossing an ocean and enduring many unspeakable sacrifices, hardships, and disappointments so my siblings and I would have a chance to live a life better than theirs.

Contents

Acknowledgments

My deepest love, admiration, and gratitude to my wife, Sylvia Tang, for her strength, love, patience, and support. If not for you, I would not be the person I am today. I will always admire your commitment to right versus wrong, your integrity, and your ride-or-die spirit.

My thanks to the countless teachers, legislative staff, advocates, labor and community leaders, and elected officials who mentored and supported me throughout my journey. To them I owe my education, inspiration, dedication, humility, compassion, and determination.

Among them, I wish to acknowledge the following (not in any particular order): Marysville High School (MHS) Football Head Coach Bob Thompson, MHS Football Coach Larry Crouch, MHS Football Coach Jac Cummings, MHS Swim Team Coach Chet Dunbar, MHS Journalism Teacher Louise Maher, MHS English Teacher Marlene Barber, MHS Debate Teacher John Collum, MHS History Teacher John Lewin, MHS Civics Teacher Bill Haggart, Jadine Chin Nielsen, Lucy McCoy, Dave and Frances Low, Georgette and Roy Imura, Maeley and Ron Tom, Jerry and Dorothy Enomoto, Hon. Norm Mineta, Hon. Robert Matsui, Hon. Hilda Solis, Hon. Judy Chu, Hon. Anthony Rendon, Hon. John Chiang, Hon. Betty Yee, Hon. Alberto Torrico, Hon. Mike Honda, Hon. Paul Fong, Hon. Warren Furutani, Hon. Russ Hom, Hon. Rick Sueyoshi, Hon. Phil Isenberg, Hon. Joe Serna, Hon. Jimmie Yee, Hon. Darrell Fong, Steve Barkan, Parke Skelton, Richie Ross, Garry South, Phil Giarrizzo,

Lenny Goldberg, Dean Tipps, Dotson Wilson, Jon Waldie, Geoff Long, John Griffing, Dolores Duran-Flores, Patrick Henning Sr., Steve Holloway, Heidi Kellison, Diane Van Maren, Pat Leary, Dan Wall, Michael Rattigan, Krist Lane, Terry Brennand, Michelle Castro, Joyce Iseri, Leah Cartebruno, Ken Topper, Steve Coony, Kathy Bowler, Nettie Sabelhaus, Danny Curtin, Ted and Michelle Toppin, Willie Pelote, Steve Smith, Kathy Mossberg, Allison Harvey, Peggy Collins, Tim Shelley, Bill Julian, Joe Caves, Peter Detwiler, Rick Simpson, Cathy Senderling-McDonald, Frank Mecca, Casey McKeever, Roger Dunstan, Gene Wong, Wendy Notsinneh, Phyllis Chow, Janet Sakata, Sherry Yee, Randy Chinn, Linda Yip, Marilyn Isenberg, Christine Minnehan, Nancy Miller, Dr. Sonney Chong, Jerry and Perla Fat, Luke and Grace Kim, Professor George Kagiwada, Professor Peter Leung, Professor Isao Fujimoto, Diane Ujiiye, Mike Watanabe, Bill Watanabe, Ford and Frances Kuramoto, Kerry Doi, Dale Minami, Don Tamaki, Alice Bulos, Cynthia Bonta, Henry Der, Margaret Iwanaga Penrose, Paul Osaki, Chewy Ito, Dean Lan, May O. Lee, Hach Yasumura, Dick Robinson, Marjorie Swartz, Barry Broad, Allen Davenport, Jim Gross, Jon Sperring, Bill Devine, and Johnnie Giles.

In addition, there are far too many friends and colleagues to list that I've had the honor to know and work with and whose support I am deeply grateful for. You've all been a treasure and I will forever be indebted to you for your kindness and inspiration.

Lastly, many thanks to my editor, David Aretha, publishing consultant, Martha Bullen, and book designer, Christy Day. You made this process easy and your expertise was critical to crafting a final product that I am tremendously proud of.

Prologue

Today would be a fight.

Simmering with silent rage and resentment, I entered the majestic conference room where this little skirmish would take place. The room was tucked in a discreet corner of a historic building anointed with marble floors, intricately carved hardwood, and oversized portraits of powerful men. Its ornately curved woodcraft; dark, rich, leather-covered hardwood chairs; blood-red carpet; and gold, tasseled, velvet curtains all disdainfully whispered to me that I didn't belong. The room was filled with graduates from the nation's most elite universities and the scions of political dynasties.

My nemesis was already in the room. He was perfect. His hair was perfect. His dark navy, pin-striped, double-breasted suit was perfect. His Ivy League education was perfect. His office placement in this elite program was perfect.

I was quite literally the opposite. I'm pretty sure my tie didn't match my blazer and my blazer didn't match my pants. My shoes came from Marshalls or Ross. I'm not sure I even owned a proper suit at the time. I barely graduated from a respectable but modest state university. I was so grateful to get into the program that I took the office placement that no one else wanted.

He stood at the head of the table preparing to serve me a deftly crafted public humiliation. I think he thought Asians were going to be an easy mark. I believe he saw this as a convenient opportunity to practice what he probably thought would be a lifetime of dominating a room and everyone in it. He looked like he was about to sit down to a nice glass of Chianti, some fava beans, and a perfectly cooked ribeye. Confident, cocky…almost predatory.

The exercise that day was a vote to pass a statement of values that he had drafted for the program. It stated that participants of this elite program should be selected in direct proportion to their ethnic percentage of the state population. It was subtle. The slight appeared benign but was obliquely malignant.

What he wanted to spotlight was that there were too many Asian Americans in the program.

We were 11% of the population but 18% of the program. There were too many of us in the program, but not enough of us to block today's vote. It's not that the Asian Americans in the program didn't support affirmative action because all of us did. We didn't want to argue against the proposed statement. It's hard to explain, but the manner in which it was presented felt like we were being singled out. Targeted because we were considered model minority sell-outs and we looked like easy pickings. We were boxed in. Helpless.

Or were we?

I heard that the legendary California Assembly Speaker Willie L. Brown once said that the only skill you need in the legislature is to be able to count to a majority. My adversary had 11 votes. Those opposed or planning to abstain from supporting the statement of values counted in at 10.

It was just a statement of values. A symbolic action with no force of law. I should have just gone along with it. But it felt personal. So either I was going to deny him this win or he was going to get the win and I would teach him a lesson in the process.

But I had to be careful. I wasn't going to get up and argue against a policy I fully supported in principle. I wasn't going to be the model minority participating in the establishment's *Hunger Games* of merit. Nor was I going to attempt to explain why this maneuver felt like a personal attack on Asian Americans.

Instead, I chose to make my point in another way. In a way that would play out in between the lines. This was going to be an intimate dance in the dark with my overconfident adversary.

As he began his presentation, I relaxed my posture and pulled out some small pieces of paper on which I scribbled short notes. Each note had the name of one of my adversary's two closest allies.

One was interested in education policy and the other was interested in the judiciary. The two were seated near, but not next to him as if to physically box in some of his swing supporters. His set-up was well-planned and tactically smart.

The meeting room was small enough that everyone could see what everyone else was doing. As he proceeded to ramble off population statistics and pontificate upon the moral importance of passing the statement of values, no one could miss me quietly handing the notes to the participants next to me to pass along to his two top lieutenants. First to my right and then to my left, these small notes marched relentlessly around the table to their intended marks.

I watched his eyes track the movement of each note as he spoke. His brow furrowed. His delivery became less confident and he was clearly distracted by my perplexing play.

The first one reached the person who was interested in education. She opened the note, read it, and then folded it back up. She looked up at me, smiled, and nodded.

The second one reached the person who was interested in the judiciary. She opened the note, read it, and then folded it back up. She looked up at me, smiled, and nodded.

In that moment, his voice faltered ever so slightly. I could see a bead of sweat form on his brow. For a brief, almost imperceptible moment, his face flushed. But it was his eyes that gave everything away.

Mike Tyson is quoted as saying, "Everyone has a plan until they get punched in the mouth."

The thing about being perfect is that it is so fragile. By definition, no deviation is too small to not ruin the perfect. So here he was in the middle of his perfectly planned play, faced with a situation he had not anticipated. Did I somehow present some unexpectedly potent argument in those diminutive notes that would pull the support of his trusted lieutenants away from him and jeopardize the victory he had so carefully prepared and fancifully imagined?

What I do know about perfect people is that they are far more concerned with not losing than they are with winning. They'd rather fold and wait for the next hand than double down. In their minds, failing in public is to be avoided at all costs.

He finished his presentation with a few minutes left in our weekly group session. He thought the vote would be a slam dunk. There was brief discussion about the merits and concerns about the proposed statement. It appeared that there was mixed support for it and no clear group mandate.

Unnerved by the possibility that he may have lost two key votes from his most trusted allies, he panicked and postponed the vote.

While no one was any wiser to what was going on between us and the statement would eventually be passed by the group, I accomplished what I wanted. I wanted to avoid a messy debate on affirmative action. More importantly, I wanted to shake his confidence and make him think twice the next time he considered mistaking Asian Americans as easy marks for his personal political games.

What was on the notes?

To the education person:

> "Hey, (name of renowned national educator) is visiting this month. Do you want to help organize something to honor him when he gets into town?"

To the judiciary person:

> "Hey, (respected SCOTUS jurist) just passed away. Do you want to help me draft a group statement in memory of his accomplishments and historical significance?"

All I needed was for him to see that these two read the notes and nodded yes to me during his presentation. The manipulation played out perfectly and I let his brain do the rest of the work for me. The human mind is predisposed to make connections even when no connection exists. I counted on him and his overactive ego to assume that the notes were about him. He assumed the reactions to the notes were connected to the discussion at hand. They sort of were, but not in the way he thought. I used the immense pressure he put on himself to force him to falter. It was political jiujitsu.

He intended to have his moment of glory at the expense of Asian Americans, and I exploited his weaknesses to take that away from him.

In today's world of performative politics, I could have made a big speech during the meeting or posted an indignant diatribe on Twitter. But this was just a game, cynically cloaked under a veil of virtue and equity messaging. Passing the statement of values would not have had any functional effect on the program's recruitment or selection process. The program was already well-known for prioritizing diversity, equity, and inclusion. This play was just a solution looking for a problem as a means to satiate someone's delicately manicured ego.

This little exercise was far better dealt with in the shadows. It was surgical and stealthy. I made my point to the person who mattered and no one else was the wiser. No unnecessary collateral damage and no evidence at the scene of the crime.

(This is a true story but some details of this story such as architectural elements and the attributes of individuals were altered to protect the identities of those involved and the program where it occurred.)

Preface

> "The two most important days in your life are the day you are born and the day you find out why."
>
> —MARK TWAIN

I was in my early teens. It was a Sunday evening and I sat cross-legged on dark green shag carpet in my childhood home's family room inches from an old 19-inch faux wood cabinet console television from Montgomery Ward. Faded Chinese porcelain figurines adorned the top of the television cabinet. So too did a can wrapped in red paper sprouting with the remnant red stems of slowly spent Chinese incense, as well as a wilting houseplant resting on a faded and water-stained dinner plate.

I sat enthralled by a Japanese television show about politics, the power and pitfalls of government, stoic heroism, and the price of pursuing the greater good. As a Chinese American growing up in a small rural community forty-five minutes north of California's Capital, this Japanese show was as close as I would get for decades to seeing someone on screen that looked like me but was not the butt of jokes or some diabolical villain.

The show was set in the Tokugawa Era of feudal Japan. The benevolent emperor had died, and the heir to the throne was his five-year old son. An Imperial Court official, Hoshina Masayuki, was chosen to serve as guardian and advisor to the young emperor as other Court nobles feigned allegiance and secretly jockeyed for power and plotted ways to usurp control of the vulnerable transitional government.

Each week, Hoshina foiled schemes to take over the government by corrupt and power-hungry politicians. He recruited the leader of a clan of exiled ninjas, Hattori Hanzo, to secretly help him mete out punishment, thwart plots against the young emperor, and protect Japan's common folk from the abuses of the rich and powerful. Both Hoshina and Hanzo stoically followed strict codes of personal conduct and acted on principle, but each also had differing agendas to serve.

Hoshina's priority was to preserve a stable nation. With the help of Hanzo and his small crew of ninjas, corrupt politicians would be punished by Hoshina but he would keep their crimes and punishment secret in order to keep the populace calm and peaceful by preserving the perception that the government was stable and free of corruption. Hanzo's priority was to protect his clan from government persecution and fight for commoners. He didn't trust the government, but worked with Hoshina when their objectives aligned with regard to rooting out corruption and protecting the safety of the public. It was a tense and often tested imperfect partnership based on principle, not on profit or power.

It wasn't the swashbuckling samurai swordplay and martial arts melees that inspired me. It was the complexity of choices that Hoshina and Hanzo had to make to stay true to their principles and their nuanced approach to government and activities outside of government to protect the people. In order to do what was right for the people while keeping within the confines of their personal code of honor, both Hoshina and Hanzo had to make tremendous sacrifices and endure many injuries and small injustices in order to serve the greater good. This appealed to me. I don't really know why, but I wanted to be what Hoshina and Hanzo were and do what they did: live by a code and work inside and outside of government to help people.

The name of the show was *Shadow Warriors*.

I recently ended a career that spanned over 30 years working in and around California's state government and on political campaigns to elect Democrats to local, state, and federal offices.

It was an improbable path for an immigrant from China like me who came with his family across an ocean with next to nothing. My father started as a cook and my mother as a waitress. As an infant, I was often strapped to her back as she took orders and delivered dishes to customers. Eventually, they owned a small restaurant that struggled to make ends meet in a small, rural town. Somehow, they endured and made enough to put a roof over our heads and send me and my siblings to college.

I didn't come from wealth or influence. I didn't even speak English when I arrived, and I didn't attend an Ivy League school or earn any advanced degrees. I only attended public schools and a public university. Yet, in the course of my career I would be working to pass laws and budgets that would impact hundreds of thousands of Californians and have opportunities to meet U.S. presidents, U.S. senators, members of U.S. Congress, state constitutional officers, state supreme court justices, legislative leaders, billionaires, and civil rights legends.

Over the last three decades, I had the honor of working for intrepid public servants who went on to become iconic political leaders. Some of these include: California State Senator Hilda L. Solis, who went on to serve in Congress and be appointed as U.S. labor secretary under President Obama; State Assemblymember Mike Honda, who went on to serve in Congress; State Assemblymember Judy Chu, who went on to become the first Chinese American woman elected to Congress and serve as the chair of the Congressional Asian Pacific American Caucus; and Assemblymember Anthony Rendon, who went on to become the longest-serving speaker of the state Assembly since Speaker Willie L. Brown.

I also lobbied for consumer ratepayers and civil rights organizations, consulted Fortune 100 companies, labor unions, and directed a political action committee that spent millions to successfully elect historic numbers of AAPIs to state legislative and constitutional seats. For nearly six years, I served as the political director for the California Assembly Democrats under Speaker Anthony Rendon and led efforts that resulted in electing the largest Assembly Democratic supermajority in over a century.

I was also able to work in the shadows and marshal a unique set of skills, powerful political relationships, and the complex levers of government to help people and support good causes.

Dream meets reality.

This book is a collection of stories about some of the experiences and lessons learned along the way.

Introduction

"It is better to be a warrior in a garden than a gardener in a war."

—BRUCE LEE

At the writing of this book, American democracy has barely survived a violent attempt to overturn a presidential election and various interests continue to use social media to undermine public confidence and trust in orderly governance. Corporate greed is widening the wealth gap, humanity faces an existential environmental climate crisis, crime and corruption continue unabated, drug addiction and homelessness afflict more and more Americans from all walks of life, middle-class families continue to struggle to make ends meet, and war and terrorism rage on in lands near and far. Asian Americans are still reeling from an unprecedented multi-year epidemic of racist hostility and violence. Civil society seems to be at the very edge of collapse.

A few years ago I boarded a plane and ran into an Asian/Latina friend who was a labor lobbyist. We chatted about the state of chaos and dysfunction of the world and how scary things were. She and her partner just had a baby and she wondered aloud how she could protect her baby from all of it.

I was silent for a moment, and then said: "You have to raise a warrior."

As we parted, I asked myself, "If I needed to raise a warrior, where would I even start? How do you even raise a warrior?"

This book is meant to provide readers my perspective on the craft and power of politics. It examines the mindset and machinery involved in the use of power, the qualities of those involved in the game, and the sacrifices necessary to affect meaningful substantive change for those who don't have a voice in the halls of power.

I wrote this book to inspire and teach ordinary people how to lead and fight.

This book is NOT about how to climb the political career ladder or seek status through pandering deference to people in positions of power. This book is about learning the skills and strategies necessary to build your own power and win the fights that matter to you.

The hope of this book is to provide practical advice and inspiration to those who care to take on fights for justice and seek to build a kinder and more responsible civilization. The book offers an alternative approach to community impact for change agents who are disillusioned by the current state of superficial social media activism, virtue signaling, political dogmatism, and performative advocacy.

In short, this book seeks to impart the skills and strategies that can help change the world in a positive way, but also to awaken the indomitable fighting spirit and stoic leadership that lies buried in the hearts of its readers.

I am also unapologetically Asian American and this book curates some key Asian American and Pacific Islander (AAPI) political stories. AAPIs need to know that we played and continue to play an important role at the table where decisions are made. These stories are meant to be a rebuke of the narrative of AAPIs as impotent and passive model minorities that mainstream journalists and entertainment media often fetishize and that many AAPIs still adopt as an acceptable depiction of their identity in America.

When I started my career in politics in 1987 there were only a handful of AAPIs in professional leadership roles and no AAPIs were serving in the California State Legislature. In fact, no AAPIs served in the California State Legislature from 1980 to 1992. As of June 2022, a historic number of AAPIs are employed in senior staff roles and hold local, state, and federal elected offices.

While some of these gains are partially a function of population growth, it's one of the objectives of this book to acknowledge the AAPIs that had the courage to run for office and the individuals and organizations that played an active and indispensable role in electing, appointing, and employing AAPIs in positions of power. If nothing else, I want the AAPI readers of this book to embrace the conviction that AAPIs are responsible for their own empowerment and representation.

The takeaway lesson is this: A seat at the table is not given. It is taken. So take it.

This book is about how to do it.

PART I

Leaders

"A man got to have a code."

—OMAR LITTLE FROM *THE WIRE*

Author Simon Sinek in his book *Leaders Eat Last* said, "If your actions inspire others to dream more, learn more, do more and become more, you are a leader." *Leaders Eat Last* refers to a practice in the U.S. Marines where Marine leaders are expected to eat last at the mess hall. Instead of being first in line for food in front of subordinates, these leaders line up behind them. The daily practice exists to emphasize and reinforce the organization's cultural code that places the needs of others ahead of one's personal needs. Sinek asserts, "Great leaders truly care about those they are privileged to lead and understand that the true cost of leadership privilege comes at the expense of self-interest."

CHAPTER 1

Character

> "I never saw a wild thing sorry for itself. A bird will fall frozen dead
> from a bough without ever having felt sorry for itself."
>
> —D.H. LAWRENCE

You can't have leadership without character. Some people believe that they become leaders when they've accumulated all the right titles and someone higher in the food chain has bestowed them the authority to lead an organization and its people. I believe that true leaders don't rely on titles or the authority of others. True leaders inspire loyalty and effort through the power of their character and the depth of their relationship with those under their responsibility. I use the word "responsibility" intentionally. The people of an organization are not under the command of a leader; they are the responsibility of the leader.

So what is character? Merriam-Webster defines character as "the complex of mental and ethical traits marking and often individualizing a person, group, or nation." Qualities that make up the character of a good leader include: humility, integrity, courage, compassion, and perseverance. Leaders with these qualities have tremendous inherent influence and impact on those within their responsibility.

I believe these qualities are instilled in a leader long before they ever assume the mantle of leadership. I also believe that these qualities are observed, adopted, and tested before they are fully manifested in a leader. Here are some of the individuals and experiences that helped to shape me as a person and prepared me for the challenges of leadership that I encountered later in my political career.

The Apology

I was a mediocre mess in high school. I was a model student on the outside, but completely lost and weak on the inside. I ran track in middle school so I tried out for track in high school during my freshman year. My rural high school was small, so it seemed that everyone always made it on the team. I was such a baby. I hated practice so I quit.

I wasn't particularly close to the coach, but his disappointment in me for quitting cut me so deep that the shame of it lingers with me to this day. It hurt because he believed in me even when I didn't believe in myself and I hated myself for that.

Subsequently, my best friend convinced me to join the junior varsity football team with him as sophomores. Again, everyone made the team and the bar was low. He was a starter; I wasn't even close. Still filled with shame and regret from quitting the track team, I vowed I would stick it out through football no matter what. I had no idea how difficult it would be to keep that vow and how being on the football team would change my life.

Football practice started in the summer with two practices a day, one in the morning and one in the late afternoon, for two weeks. I think we called them "Hell Weeks." The temperatures during the summers in the small town I grew up in would regularly exceed 100 degrees. I had never played organized football before. I didn't even watch games on TV. I had no idea what I was doing and I was far behind all my teammates in skill, speed, and endurance. I was by far the worst player on the team. I dreaded every practice. I dreaded it so much that I would get to the field an hour…sometimes two hours… early and stare at the field just to build up the courage to suit up and struggle through each practice. It's hard for me to say which was the worst aspect of summer practice…the heat or the humiliation. Most days, I would wish that I'd get hit by a car on my way to practice so I would have a legitimate excuse to skip it.

Somehow I made it through the junior varsity season and signed up again for varsity the following year. Again, making it on the team was basically automatic. On varsity, the high school juniors played with the high school seniors. Our star running back was senior classman Al Perez. He was popular, a top student in academics headed for UC Berkeley, and dating one of the most popular cheerleaders in school. In my mind, he had it all.

One day our team had a particularly bad practice. It was apocalyptically hot. Just breathing was hard. We were all tired and unmotivated. We just wanted to get through the practice and forget it even happened. The head coach had us run plays at the end of practice and everyone kept making mistakes. The more mistakes we made, the angrier and louder the coaches got. It was just bad all around, and the frustration among the coaches and the players was uncomfortably palpable. On one of the final plays, the center—a kid named Jimmy—made a blocking mistake and Al Perez completely lost it and verbally blew up at Jimmy. Al never lost his temper. Today he did. It was a tense moment…like when your parents are fighting and you'd do anything to not be in the house.

Jimmy was not a star player on the team or an academic standout. He was quiet and hardworking. He apologized repeatedly on the field to Al and you could see he felt horrible about missing the block and letting down his teammates. Al just walked away from Jimmy. The awkwardness of the situation hung over all of us like a heavy wool blanket on top of the stifling late afternoon heat and the stench of our sweat-soaked practice jerseys. Seeing that no good would come from continuing this practice session, the coaches called it a day and sent us to the locker room to pack it in.

What happened next changed everything for me.

The locker room was deafeningly quiet as players put away their gear and packed their gym bags. It smelled like sweat, grass stains, and dirt. No one was talking and all heads were down. The coaches walked straight to their offices and slammed their doors with a loud bang. All you could hear was clicking combination locks, squeaking locker doors, and zipping gym bags.

Jimmy was seated on a bench in the middle of the room, head down. Defeated. Helmet at his side, shoulder pads at his feet. No one looked at him.

Al came in and went up to Jimmy and said, "Hey, Jimmy, I'm sorry. I shouldn't have went off on you like that." Al didn't whisper it, nor did he say it loudly as if it were some magnanimous pronouncement. He said it earnestly and confidently, man to man.

It was a quiet and touching moment.

Al was the star of the team. He was an academic standout accepted to Cal. He was dating a cheerleader. None of us would have even thought about criticizing him for losing his temper at Jimmy. Yet Al took it upon himself to genuinely apologize to Jimmy in full view of everyone in the locker room.

I was only a few feet away. In complete awe of the moment, I remember thinking to myself, *Wow. I hope one day to be big enough to do what he just did.*

After decades of working with politicians who are looked to as leaders, I can say that the vast majority of them fail miserably when it comes to apologies. Leaders aren't perfect and when they make a mistake they need to be able to honestly own it. Either their ego is too big to admit it or they are poorly staffed by consultants that mistakenly believe a cleverly written pivot will deescalate the situation. Trust me, just own it and take your lumps like an adult.

While what Al did was a powerful act of character and leadership, the actions that really changed me came from Jimmy. He was a second-string player on a team that hadn't had a winning season in nearly a decade. There wasn't much at stake when he made the wrong block on a shitty practice day. The mistake didn't cost us a win or a championship. But you wouldn't know it by watching Jimmy. He carried that mistake like a giant boulder on his shoulders. He was harder on himself than Al or the coaches were on him. He was a true believer in the game and the team.

Up until that moment, I was just on the team to wear a jersey and add another activity to my college application. I didn't believe in the game or the team. On that day, Jimmy taught me that being a winner is not about being on a winning team. Being a winner is believing in the game and the team…no matter what. Own your role. How you conduct yourself in these moments is far more important than the score at the end of a game or the win-loss record at the end of the season.

I reflect often about that day and try to live up to the lessons on leadership and character taught to me by Al and Jimmy on the field and in that locker room.

Challenge Day

As I said before, I was easily the worst player on the team. So how could I contribute without being on the field on game night?

It was my senior year and the Marysville High School football team had gone nearly a decade without a winning season. There was a time when even some of the cheerleaders openly said we couldn't win. We felt like losers and played like losers. We played poorly against teams we could beat and played well when overmatched, but never well enough to win. We couldn't close. We needed to have more grit and character if we wanted to go the distance and win games.

I was never a starter. I wasn't even second string and we didn't have enough players for a legitimate third string. I had nothing to contribute on the field on game day, but maybe I had something I could contribute on the field during practice. Thursday practices were light to make sure our starters would be fresh for the Friday night games. As part of the effort to fire up the team before game day, we ended Thursdays with a challenge drill. Any player could challenge any other player on the team to a head-to-head tackle. Each player squared off in the three-point stance about three yards apart, and at the whistle they would take a go at each other with the intent to deliver the hardest hit they could.

I was tired of losing. I was angry and frustrated. I wanted our team to rise up and show the school and the league we had the hearts of winners and we weren't afraid of anyone. So on one Thursday and every other Thursday during the season, I would challenge the biggest, toughest players on the team.

I guess I could've worried about looking like a chump and a loser, taking on someone bigger and stronger than me. Maybe it would have been more macho to take on the smallest person on the team and crush him into the ground (not possible because I was literally the smallest person on the team). Not that it was uncommon for some of the bigger players to pick smaller players. We were in high school. Immature, hormone-driven shit like that happened all the time.

I'd get creamed every time. Completely obliterated. You could hear the crack of the hit all across the field and bounce off the windows of the classrooms two blocks away. At first it was funny and cringy. I'd often end up on the bottom of a 300-pound lineman or a 225-pound linebacker in a crumpled, 135-pound heap of sweat and grass stains. But then I'd get up. Every time. Defiant.

Nelson Mandela once said, "Do not judge me by my successes. Judge me by how many times I fell down and got back up again."

I couldn't play well, but I could try to lead by example. My message to my teammates was that this team never gives up, even if we face a bigger or better person on the other side of the line. It didn't matter how many times we failed before or failed after. It was about character. The lesson also was that sometimes you have got to take one for the team.

I can't say for sure that my weekly self-immolation made the difference, but team members started going the extra mile, fighting for that extra inch, taking hits for each other so we could get the ball into the end zone. We never gave up on a game or each other again. We started to feel like a real team…a team that coincidentally started winning games. We ended the season tied for third in the league and with the best school record in nearly a decade.

The experience taught me that every player on the team has something to contribute. You don't have to be named team captain to take on the responsibility to lead when the chips are down, and it's the little things that you do that can inspire and encourage the best from those around you.

At the end of the season, my teammates voted me MHS Varsity Football's Most Inspirational Player. Head coach Bob Thompson wrote in my yearbook, "To one of the most inspirational people I ever met. I know you will do well so you don't need to be wished any luck!"

These lessons stuck with me my entire life and would come into play years later when I was chief of staff to Assemblywoman Judy Chu and the political director of the Assembly Democrats.

Office Space

When California's 66th speaker of the Assembly, Fabian Nunez, appointed Chu to chair the Assembly Appropriations Committee, not only did she inherit the most powerful committee in the Assembly, she inherited one of the most impressive offices in the Capitol Building. I served as her chief of staff and historically would have inherited the coveted staff office outside her personal office. In addition, there would typically be jostling between the chair's personal staff and the committee staff for prime office space.

Chairwoman Chu had very ambitious policy goals and needed the best around her to achieve those goals. As chief, I was charged with helping her reach those goals. After reviewing the staff roster and the chairwoman's legislative priorities, I knew that having a committee staff fully onboard would be a critical step toward achieving her goals. I went to the committee's chief consultant, Geoff Long, and offered him an office placement plan that favored his staff over mine. Chairwoman Chu had a very aggressive plan to fight to protect and expand state healthcare, so I gave up what would have been my office next to her office to Scott Bain, the Appropriations Committee health policy expert, so that she could have quick and convenient access to his encyclopedic knowledge of state health policy and budget funding.

I could have just taken another one of the staff offices, but instead I prioritized other staff. Eventually I took the back corner office (the furthest office from the chairwoman's office) with no windows and shared it with the chairwoman's senior assistant, Chinook Shin, who was the operational glue of the office. We were the two most senior members of the chairwoman's personal staff roster and we made the biggest sacrifice in office space.

The sacrifice did not go unnoticed. The camaraderie between the personal staff and committee staff was unprecedented. Many of the committee staffers took Chu's personal staff under their wings and helped them along in their legislative careers. The friendships forged during this time endure today. Chu was able to benefit greatly from the vast knowledge and skill of the committee staff to overcome some of the most difficult budget funding decisions faced by the Assembly and pass landmark legislation to benefit Californians from all walks of life all across the state.

Unsurprisingly, some of the attention was negative. The talk around the Capitol was that Geoff overruled me on office assignments and that I did not exert myself aggressively enough as Judy's chief of staff. Not that Geoff couldn't have rolled me if he wanted to. He was literally a legend in the Capitol. Rolling me would have been child's play for him. He knew the building better than anyone and was unafraid to play hardball if necessary. Instead, he was quite gracious and accommodating. Nevertheless, it would have been petty to choose office space based on perception and contrary to the best interest of the chairwoman, so Chinook and I decided to take one for the team.

My play was for the long game. That's why the rumor didn't bother me in the least. If anything, I was amused by it. It obviously came from the small-minded elements of the Capitol community that are obsessed with petty dick-measuring exercises. In the end, my respect for Geoff and his staff only grew and I learned a tremendous amount from them. More importantly, Geoff and the committee staff helped deliver the groundbreaking legislative successes for Chu that earned her the support of voters and editorial boards that would be critical to her successful runs for state constitutional officer and the United States House of Representatives.

Assembly Required

In 2017, Speaker Anthony Rendon entrusted me with running the Assembly Democrats. This is the arm of the California Democratic Party responsible for holding and growing the Assembly's Democratic majority. In 2016, high presidential Democratic turnout helped the Assembly Democrats win back seats that were lost in 2014's low-turnout midterm election, but the organization was recovering from dysfunctional management and some structural obsolescence. In 2018 we were headed into another potentially low-turnout midterm election that threatened to result in Democratic losses.

We had just renewed our lease and reconfigured the Assembly Democrats office into an open space concept. We also ordered 25 new adjustable-height desks from IKEA to replace the rummage sale furniture from the 1970s that usually occupies a campaign office. Like all IKEA products, these desks were delivered as "assembly required."

Instead of spending precious campaign funds paying for IKEA's assembly services or asking the current Assembly Democrats finance staff (our only full-time staff) to assemble the desks, I spent several weekends assembling the desks myself with the occasional help of my close friend and staff colleague, John Nam, who was chief of staff to the first Native American elected to the state Assembly, James Ramos. He's a leader that has a huge heart who is willing to take on any task to help the team no matter how small. It's these same qualities that have won him the respect of his colleagues and earned him his current high-level job of deputy secretary of the California Senate. We assembled 25 desks in all. It cost me some intense mental aggravation (thanks to IKEA's infamously cryptic assembly manuals), a little personal time, and two or three pizzas and a few six-packs of beer.

I wanted to send a message to the staff and legislative leadership that no one, not even the political director, is above doing the grunt work necessary to spend our money wisely and win the races that would allow us to hold or grow the Assembly's Democratic majority. Once the desks were assembled and arranged, I chose to sit at one in the open space instead of taking one of the private offices in the suite. Again, I thought it was important for me to show my respect, deference, and accessibility to the staff doing the day-to-day work to elect more Democrats.

I also walked precincts and phone-banked. This was above and beyond my job description. At 208 hours in 2018, I put in more walking and phone bank hours than any other volunteer and any previous political director. I walked in places like Jurupa Valley, Corona, Santa Clarita, Dublin, San Bernardino, Bakersfield, and Hanford. I walked some sketchy-ass neighborhoods, dodged some large, unleashed dogs, seen more chain link fencing than I care to admit, talked to frustrated and hostile voters, got chased out of mobile home parks, snuck into gated communities, stayed at shitty hotels, ate day-old campaign food, and got drunk at the local dive bars just like everyone else on the campaign. It was so epically fun. Really, it was glorious. No, I'm serious. Really.

I wasn't going to ask anyone to do anything I wouldn't do myself, and I didn't just hang out at campaign HQ trying to look busy and avoid eye contact with volunteers. I grabbed a kit, sometimes two, and headed out to work a precinct. With the Political Data Inc. (PDI) GPS-enabled mobile app that's used by campaigns for tracking door-to-door voter contact, it's easy to spot someone posting up at a local watering hole and filling in the surveys. I was glad that campaign staff would be tracking my door knocks and calling behind me to voters to verify contact.

Having once been a young staff volunteer, I hated it when I saw senior staff post up at the HQ or pick up a kit and then half-ass the precinct walk. Sometimes we would see them parked at a bar until it was time to bring the kits back in. I never understood it. There was always time to get drunk *after* getting some good precinct walking war stories. Some of my best times working a precinct were spent with OG chiefs like Tom White and John Ferrera.

In 2016 we volunteered on Sharon Quirk-Silva's tough re-elect in Orange County. She had been elected in 2012 in an upset race that flipped a Republican seat only to lose the seat in 2014 due to extremely low Democratic midterm turnout.

Evan McLaughlin, a young but exceptionally skilled chief of staff in the Assembly, was running the ground operation and dubbed us three "the Council of Elders" because we were the oldest staffers on the volunteer crew. The name kind of stung, but I can't say he was wrong. To this day, we occasionally reconvene the "Council of Elders" at a bar near the capitol to recount our favorite campaign horror stories and grouse about old age and lazy staffers.

During the last four days of the campaign, we'd spend the day walking precincts to turn out Democratic voters and late evenings prepping kits for the next day or tidying up the campaign office. Both Tom and John were legendary chiefs of staff, respected in the building, and admired by their employees. They could have easily pulled rank and picked much easier assignments by the beach and no one would have questioned them.

But there they were, grinding out votes in Stanton and taking on the hills in Santa Ana. On election night, we were walking precincts in the dark at 7:45 p.m. to get voters to their polls before they closed at 8 p.m. As long as voters were in line by 8 p.m., they'd still be allowed to cast their votes. We stayed at polling stations until about 9 p.m. to make sure everyone who was in line was allowed to vote. It was a great team effort that produced a win for Quirk-Silva that brought her back to Sacramento and the state Assembly.

Two years later in 2018, the "Council of Elders" reunited in Bakersfield and Hanford to help re-elect Rudy Salas, who was a perennial Republican Party target and facing a multimillion-dollar dark money attack funded by industrial agricultural interests. At one point, we worked out of a small and ramshackle "inn" that was converted from a burned-out orphanage. The vibe was *The Shining* meets *The Addams Family*. There was a small child's handprint on the wall next to the front desk that the manager said was impossible to remove or paint over. We heard stories of doors that opened by themselves and strange noises at night. Despite the challenging experience presented by the creepy orphan inn, Salas survived the tough re-elect with the help of the Council of Elders and a small army of determined volunteers.

By the end of 2018 in what was expected to be a low-turnout midterm election unfavorable to Democrats like 2014, Assembly Speaker Anthony Rendon and Assembly Democrats' Finance Director David Pruitt had raised a record-breaking campaign war chest that funded a field of outstanding Democratic candidates. Meanwhile, the rest of the team rallied with innovative tactics and organized a massive volunteer effort that won five additional Democratic seats and gave the Assembly's Democratic Caucus its largest majority in over 130 years. Two years later in 2020, the same team overcame the COVID-19 shutdown and severely limited door-to-door voter contact to hold every incumbent seat in the Assembly's Democratic mega-majority. These victories significantly increased the ethnic and gender diversity in the Assembly and laid the groundwork for the historic gains made by women candidates elected to the legislature in 2022.

Under Speaker Rendon, the Assembly delivered the most progressive policy agenda in the history of the state by passing unprecedented state investments in housing construction and transportation infrastructure, the toughest anti-tobacco laws in the nation, the toughest gun safety laws in the nation, and world-leading policies on greenhouse gas and carbon emission reductions. The state Assembly under Rendon's leadership strongly supported efforts that made California the only state in the nation to pass overtime pay for farm workers and the first state in the nation to pass the $15 minimum wage.

CHAPTER 2

Vision

"A leader is one who sees more than others see, who sees farther than others see, and who sees before others see."

—LEROY EIMES

Steve Jobs once said:

> You can't connect the dots looking forward; you can only connect them looking backwards. So you have to trust that the dots will somehow connect in your future. You have to trust in something—your gut, destiny, life, karma, whatever. This approach has never let me down, and it has made all the difference in my life.

In the movie *Any Given Sunday*, Al Pacino's character gives his team an inspiring halftime speech that includes the following passage:

> You find out life's this game of inches. So is football because in either game, life or football, the margin for error is so small. I mean, one half a step too late or too early and you don't quite make it. One half second, too slow, too fast, you don't quite catch it. The inches we need are everywhere around us. They're in every break of the game, every minute, every second. On this team, we fight for that inch. On this team, we tear ourselves and everyone else around us to pieces for that inch. We claw with our fingernails for that inch because we know when we add up

all those inches, that's going to make the fucking difference between winning and losing, between living and dying.

What most people miss is that you've got to be looking for the dots and those inches. They're all around us. If you want to be a great leader and you want to innovate and inspire, then you need to learn to seek the hidden gems, undervalued players, and overlooked opportunities. Too much of current leadership training focuses on following a fixed formula for success and pandering to the wealthy and powerful to attain status. Doing so intrinsically makes you a follower, not a leader.

In the Land of the Blind, the One-Eyed Man Is King

I'm a huge fan of *Star Trek*, the original series. My favorite episode is "Arena," which aired in Season 1. In this episode, Captain Kirk and the reptilian captain of an opposing alien ship are stranded on a barren planet by a superior life form. The life form tells the two captains that there is a weapon on the planet that will allow one of them to destroy the other. The combatant who finds the weapon and destroys his opponent will be spared and returned to his ship.

Kirk is physically outmatched by the giant reptile captain. Desperate, Kirk spends most of the episode escaping and evading his opponent in a frantic effort to find the weapon before his opponent finds it. Kirk traverses the deserted terrain only to come across bamboo, diamonds, coal, sulfur, and some twine—all items that fail to be useful against his thick-skinned adversary.

Eventually, Kirk realizes that he can combine all these "useless" things he has come across and build a makeshift cannon to defeat the physically superior alien captain.

The point is that if you want to accomplish something that hasn't been done before, you can't do it by using the same thinking and theories that led you to where you are now. Thomas Edison did not find a light bulb in a tree and Steve Jobs did not trip over an iPhone on a weekend safari. They cobbled together knowledge and resources to make something completely new and revolutionary.

If you want to be a leader you are going to encounter many difficult situations and vexing decisions. While it's important to know and use history as a guide, it's even more important to understand how to use that knowledge in context of what you are facing and what you want to accomplish. Leaders need to be able to recognize elements and qualities that may seem useless initially but could be critical pieces of a solution and to improvise and think unconventionally in order to overcome unexpected or unique challenges.

Leaders need to be effective in building coalitions and crafting compromises in order to successfully change the world. To do so, leaders should spend less time on what they're saying and more time hearing what the person on the other side of the table is trying to tell them. It's easier than one might think.

I speak on a lot of panels about legislative advocacy and how to be better legislative staff. One of the lobbying tips I give them is to look around the office of the person they are lobbying. I tell them to ask, "What is this person telling me?" Do they like sports, musical theater, superheroes, animals? Are they religious?" A person's office is very personal. They decorate it with the things that remind them of what's important to them or demonstrate what interests, inspires, or compels them. This is them telling anyone who comes in who they are and what's important to them. It's social signaling.

Once I've "heard" what they're trying to tell me, I then tune my pitch to match the tone and tenor of their voice. If they're sports fans, I use sports analogies. If they like superheroes, I describe my proposal in terms of the hero's journey. If they're religious, I try to find the appropriate faith references that can bridge gaps in perspective and understanding.

Ripples to Riptide

The Butterfly Effect is a concept in Chaos Theory that suggests the flapping wings of a butterfly somewhere can result in a typhoon somewhere else that is far, far away. Mastering politics is all about understanding how a concept like this can come into play and how important the long game is.

In the late 1980s I was an intern in a tiny office that was at one time a utility closet. Inside this obscure and cramped little cubby hole sat two of the most powerful and courageous AAPI women I will have ever met.

Maeley Tom and Georgette Imura ran the Office of Asian Pacific Islander Affairs for California Senate President Pro Tem David Roberti. Maeley was the first AAPI and woman to serve as the chief administrative officer of the state Assembly and then served as chief of staff to state Senate President Pro Tempore David Roberti. Georgette had worked for powerhouse legislators like Julian Dixon and Yvonne Brathwaite Burke.

In this internship I became a skilled delivery boy and expert at sifting through newspapers from all across the nation to curate an extensive codex of articles chronicling the efforts and issues most important to AAPIs. Translated, that meant that I spent hours with scissors, glue sticks, and a copy machine. I loved it. It gave me a window to all the things AAPIs were doing and some of the racism they faced. I was an angry and radical campus and ethnic studies activist at the time. This internship gave me context and validation. It was here that I would learn three lessons: 1) if you want respect, no one gets a pass; 2) you need to know the rules before you break the rules; and 3) organize, organize, and then organize some more.

California State Treasurer Jesse "Big Daddy" Unruh had just passed away and his office was vacant. The state treasurer's office had become extremely powerful under Unruh…possibly only second in power to the governor.

The governor had the power to appoint Unruh's replacement and he chose Congressman Dan Lungren. As a congressman, Lungren had been a vocal opponent of redress for the surviving members of the 120,000 Japanese Americans who were unconstitutionally incarcerated during World War II.

So these two petite AAPI women and a group of AAPI leaders took it upon themselves to deal out some justice and block Lungren's appointment. Let me emphasize that they led a public effort against the wishes of the popular sitting governor of the largest state of the nation at a time when no AAPI served in the state legislature.

Maeley and Georgette set about organizing AAPI civil rights leaders and the few AAPI elected officials across the country. The dynamic duo also relied on political relationships with Black and Latino leaders that they built over the years to urge key state senators to oppose ratifying Lungren's gubernatorial appointment. The sheer courage, skill, and intensity of the effort was breathtaking, and I had a courtside seat. I got to watch them organize AAPI leaders and organizations, call in favors from powerful political allies, and craft and manage media messaging that were key to obliterating Lungren's ability to be appointed. The whole thing was masterful… and successful. Lungren's appointment was defeated by the margin of a single vote cast by San Francisco state Senator Quentin Kopp.

These two women risked their careers and the livelihood of their families in taking on this fight. Yet they never wavered. Not once.

Keep in mind that at this time AAPIs were either ignored in mainstream media or portrayed as impotent and subservient sub-humans living in someone else's country. The model minority myth was in full effect. AAPIs would prosper only if they went along to get along. Asian Americans were relentlessly indoctrinated with a mindset to not rock the boat or be the nail that gets hammered down.

But here were these two AAPI women, no taller than five-foot-four, taking on the governor of California and the Republican Party's heir apparent to the office that controlled the state's massive bank account. Seeing this challenged everything I was being programmed to be as an Asian American. The experience freed me from the chains of what white society was telling me I needed to conform to. They taught me that Asian Americans need not fear anyone nor defer to anyone and that Asian Americans could hold tremendous political power if they worked together. They persisted before #shepersisted. Georgette, in her inimitable wry way, would often say, "I'm not a big shot. I'm just a little shot that keeps on shootin'."

Their actions would send a thunderclap through national political circles. In Maeley Tom's memoir, *I'm Not Who You Think I Am*, she recounted a *Washington Post* story that declared, "The sudden emergence of Asian American influence in the Lungren controversy is the most obvious of several signs of the growing political clout for a minority with only 7 percent of the state's population. In the last few months, they have revolutionized the image of what was once California's quietist minority."

More importantly, the lessons learned in this little uprising would come into play many years later and produce political dividends for the AAPI community far beyond what Maeley and Georgette ever imagined.

They used their knowledge and relationships subsequently to help Matt Fong, the Republican son of former Democratic Assemblywoman and Secretary of State March Fong Eu, to secure the votes in the state Senate necessary to approve his appointment to the state Board of Equalization. Fong would go on to serve as state treasurer and eventually unsuccessfully run for U.S. Senate against Democrat Barbara Boxer.

Half a decade later, California State Board of Equalization Member Brad Sherman was elected to the United States Congress. This left a vacancy in the state's quasi-judicial constitutional office in charge of a large portion of California's sales and property tax adjudication. It's an obscure but powerful office that serves also as a launching pad for higher office. At the time, John Chiang was Sherman's chief deputy and by law he would serve as the acting Board member for Sherman's seat on the Board until the governor appointed a replacement. A state senator was being considered for appointment by the governor. The state Senate is an intensely collegial body and it would have been easy for senators to support a Republican gubernatorial appointment from its own ranks regardless of partisan affiliation.

However, John Chiang wanted to keep the job as the acting Board member and be able to use the title to run for the office's full term in 1998. Winning the seat would give him ten years in elected office representing the politically powerful and Democratically dominated region bordered all within Los Angeles County. Serving as the Board of Equalization member representing Los Angeles County would provide the springboard for Chiang to eventually win an election as state controller and state treasurer and become a legitimate contender for governor.

Blocking the Senate from approving the appointment of a state senator to Sherman's Board of Equalization seat would be critical to the advancement of Chiang and the political aspirations of AAPIs in California. Unlike the era in which Maeley Tom and Georgette Imura served, the Legislature now had two AAPIs serving in the state Assembly. Oxnard Mayor Nao Takasugi was a Japanese American Republican elected to the Assembly in 1992. And with the help of Maeley Tom and Georgette Imura, Santa Clara County Supervisor Mike Honda was elected to the state Assembly in 1996.

Honda was a protégé of legendary Congressman Norm Mineta, who taught him the importance of building a political pipeline for AAPIs. As an assemblymember, Honda took on the challenge of blocking the governor's nomination for the Sherman vacancy. I was his legislative director at the time. We replicated the game plan that

Maeley and Georgette engineered to block Lungren to ward off the Senate nominee.

The one variation we had to address was whether the Assembly could play a role in blocking a Senate ratification. What we found was that an appointment could be blocked by either house. If the Assembly was poised to block, the Senate would not go through the political embarrassment of considering a nominee that would be blocked by the lower house.

Honda set out to lobby his colleagues in the Assembly and his office became the war room for Chiang, much like how the tiny office in the Senate served as the war room to block Lungren. Honda relentlessly cajoled his colleagues to support Chiang and persistently outmaneuvered those seeking to secure the seat for the governor's choice. Honda's determination paid off and he was able to run out the clock and block a vote to ratify a governor-nominated replacement for Sherman. The regular session of the legislature ended with Chiang firmly in place as the acting Board of Equalization member representing Southern California.

But that's not the end of this story. A little over half a decade later, Carol Migden vacated her seat on the Board of Equalization to serve in the state Senate. Her chief deputy at the time was Betty Yee, and the operation to block a gubernatorial nomination was underway once again. This time, Yee had the benefit of her mentor, Carol Migden, running the block on the Senate side, and the new chair of the AAPI Legislative Caucus, Judy Chu, running the block on the Assembly side.

As Chu's chief of staff at the time, all I needed to do was dust off the Lungren and Chiang playbook. Yee went on to hold the Board of Equalization seat easily and eventually was elected to serve as state controller after Chiang was termed out. With the help of Chiang and Yee, State Assemblymember Chu would be elected to the Board of Equalization to replace Chiang and State Assemblymember Fiona

Ma would be elected to replace Yee on the Board of Equalization. Chu would later be elected to U.S. Congress and Ma would be elected state treasurer when Chiang was termed out and running for governor.

The ripple made by two small but mighty women's plucky political effort to block an outspoken opponent of justice for Japanese Americans rolled into a mighty riptide, carrying five AAPIs to state constitutional office and the first Chinese American woman to the United States House of Representatives.

PART II

Judy Chu: Taking a Seat at the Table

"There are a lot of sharks in the world. If you hope to complete the swim, you will have to deal with them. So if you want to change the world, don't back down from the sharks."

—ADMIRAL WILLIAM H. MCRAVEN, U.S. NAVY

Some say that Viking conquerors would land on a beach and burn their boats on the shore before going into battle. The alleged reason was that they would arrive to conquer or perish. I don't know if this is true, but I took the lesson to heart and applied it to my approach to campaigns. Or as my mentor, Jadine Chin Nielsen, who worked for legendary U.S. Senator Alan Cranston and served as deputy mayor of Los Angeles, once said to me, "If you're going to pick a side, it's better to win."

It's no secret that the media and entertainment industry portray Asian Americans as weak and submissive. Nowhere is the impact of this cultural gaslighting more evident than in the arena of politics. In the decades I've worked in politics, the refrain that Asian Americans can't win races or are not leadership material is heard or implied often. At the same time, the Asian American candidates that I often deal with have a fundamental misunderstanding of what it takes to win a campaign or survive a real political fight.

Political fights are dirty. They are not spelling contests or beauty pageants. Their perfectly manicured Ivy League education, weekends in the military reserve, and brief White House internship do not guarantee them a seat in the U.S. Senate or House of Representatives. Everything that Asian Americans have been taught about leadership and success is wrong when it comes to politics. Politics has been called a knife fight in a phone booth. Some consultants literally just make shit up to win a race and they have no qualms about digging deep into your life and burning your reputation to the ground with innuendo and exaggeration.

I got good at politics by volunteering for every shit job in a campaign I could get and attending as many trainings and conferences I could find. I've participated as a volunteer or paid staff on hundreds of campaigns. There's always something new to learn and you can never get enough practice hours in, whether it was digging in trash cans for opposition research or tracking mail for the mail tree, assembling field kits, or stocking the campaign office. Every task gives you the opportunity to see and experience the mechanics of a campaign. I wanted to know how to run a campaign from soup to nuts.

I sat in every meeting I could get in on, and instead of trying to be the smartest person in the room I STFU and listened so I could learn how things were done right. If you're talking, you're not listening. I really hated sitting in campaign meetings where some snot-nosed hotshot with aspirations of becoming a chief of staff or the next Richie Ross would have to pipe in their opinion or snark every few seconds in an effort to impress the general consultant or the candidate. If you're doing this, you're not impressing anyone. You're just being a pain in the ass to the people who have things to do.

While the stories of Asian Americans winning big political fights might be few, they do exist. The following stories curate some of the big, nasty fights that have been won and what it took to win them. For those who believe elections don't matter, these stories demonstrate the importance of winning and the impact of political representation.

More importantly, the following stories are about how to win hardball campaigns where underhanded and often unethical tactics are employed. I don't go into all of the specifics because readers should just understand that lies will be made and people will be leveraged in campaigns. It's just how campaigns are played and there are no referees. I want readers to focus on the preparation, resilience, resourcefulness, and strategies that can be used to overcome an opponent with better odds or more institutional support. Better strategy, tactics, and execution are the key to winning races that are fought in the mud. If you are expecting and preparing yourself for a fair fight, all you're doing is bringing a knife to a gunfight. That's a fight you're going to lose. So be prepared for the worst or don't get in the fight at all.

In each of the following stories, Judy Chu faced extraordinary odds and entrenched institutional opposition. There was racism and sexism. There were many bad days when the outcome seemed bleak, betrayals were common, and friends were hard to find. But she prevailed each time because she and her team were always prepared, never gave up, and never backed down.

But it's not just about winning a campaign. Once she won her races, she took on those same challenges in the policy arena to overcome powerful special interests and entrenched agendas. And then she prepared for the next campaign. When the campaign is over, that's when the real work begins.

CHAPTER 3

2001 Assembly Campaign

"The acquaintance of honorable people, even at a distance, does not add flowers in times of warmth and does not change its leaves in times of cold: it continues unfading through the four seasons, becomes increasingly stable as it passes through ease and danger."

—ZHUGE LIANG

I was a staffer for California State Senator Hilda Solis in 2000 when she decided to take on 18-year incumbent U.S. Congressman Marty Martinez in the Democratic Primary. Solis was a champion for increasing the state minimum wage and backed by organized labor that wanted a stronger pro-labor champion in Congress instead of Martinez. The campaign was grueling and difficult. Despite labor's strong support, many entities and individuals were reluctant to back the young female state senator over a seasoned incumbent congressman.

Solis prevailed over Martinez in an upset, and her vacant state Senate seat would set into motion an opportunity for Monterey Park Mayor Judy Chu to vie for a seat in the state Assembly. State Assemblymember Gloria Romero, whose district overlapped parts of Solis' state Senate district, announced that she would run to replace Solis. If Romero were to be successful in the special election for Senate, Chu would be able to run for her Assembly seat in a subsequent special election.

Chu, a popular city council member/mayor and former school board member in the heart of the Assembly district, had lost two previous attempts to serve in the state Assembly. The district had a significant Asian American population, but not enough to overcome the larger and more politically sophisticated Latino population. Chu was an impressive campaigner and was able to raise significant sums of campaign cash from the district's affluent Asian American population. No matter how much money she raised, the numerical voter advantage that Latinos had in this district was virtually insurmountable.

However, Chu's supporters hypothesized that the numerical advantage would be mitigated by reduced Latino turnout in a special election scenario. They guessed that there would be Latino voter fatigue from the Solis primary election, the 2000 general election, the state Senate special election, and then finally the state Assembly special election. In contrast, they believed that Asian American voters would be highly motivated to elect an Asian American to the state Assembly and would be less fatigued because they weren't as heavily targeted for voter contact as Latino voters were in the prior elections.

Initially Chu was reluctant to mount another campaign after suffering two devastating losses in this district. But the time for her to decide was shortened because of the accelerated special election schedule. In order to force a vacancy in the Assembly seat she wanted, she would have to help Gloria Romero win the state Senate seat. Chu would eventually have to dig deep to help Romero by setting aside the bitter aftertaste of losing a hard-fought campaign against her for the same Assembly seat two years prior. Chu would also have to blindly trust that Romero would set aside the past to support her for the Assembly seat. With the help of Solis and Chu, Romero won the state Senate special election and set into motion a new special election for her vacant Assembly seat.

Chu went on to announce her run for the vacant Assembly seat but it would hardly be a cakewalk. In fact, it became more acrimonious than expected. Some state Latino leaders asserted that this was a Latino seat and recruited a Latino councilmember in the district to run against Chu. Chu's record of championing Latino issues and supporting Latino candidates like Solis was not enough to win her the support of these Latino leaders. In addition, Chu's opponent had the support of the powerful speaker of the state Assembly.

At the time, Latino political power was on the rise while Asian American political power was in its infancy. At best, Asian American political support was feeble and erratic. So much so that when I brought up my support for Chu to an Asian American Capitol staffer that was many years my senior, she tilted her head back, looked down her nose at me, and scoffed, "Judy? She can't win." I was so enraged that I made it my personal mission to help Chu win this seat.

Using my years of knowledge of the Capitol's insider political machinery and relationships I had carefully cultivated while working for Solis and Honda, I helped Chu secure meetings with lobbyists and labor leaders in Sacramento. These meetings would at best help to bring in fresh financial support or at worst convince them to stay out of the race. Having worked for Solis and Honda, I knew exactly the right words to use when meeting with these political power brokers and was able to help Chu navigate many political landmines or exploit any opportunities that presented themselves in these meetings.

Accompanying Chu to these meetings and organizing Sacramento fundraisers for her drew attention to me and resulted in some unpleasant tension between me and some of my Latino colleagues who worked for the Speaker. At that point I had already burned my boats on the shore, so it was an either conquer or die situation. And I wasn't ready to die…or let Chu lose.

As Jadine said, "Better to win."

A few additional factors came into play that would change the trajectory of this race from the races she failed to win previously.

The biggest difference in this campaign from her previous efforts was the support of Congresswoman Hilda Solis. Solis had just beaten a congressman in the only primary election upset in the nation. She was also feted nationally as the first Latina to be awarded the John F. Kennedy Profile in Courage Award for her work on landmark environmental legislation as a state senator. Her name and popularity at the time rivaled that of the legendary Los Angeles Supervisor Gloria Molina in this district.

Chu had played a pivotal role in Solis' victory over Martinez. While Solis and Martinez would fight to a virtual draw on winning Latino votes, Chu's popularity with Asian American voters in the district would provide the margin of victory in favor of Solis. Solis reciprocated and her powerful endorsement brought in game-changing support for Chu from influential labor leaders and significant segments of Latino voters in the district.

Solis' support also allowed Chu to retain Parke Skelton and Steve Barkan, who were the masterminds of Solis' upset victory over Marty Martinez. They were among the best consultants in the state and had a reputation of winning tough races on behalf of progressive candidates. Unlike many of their competitors at the time, Parke and Steve utilized granular data and exceptionally bespoke mail to surgically target and turn out pivotal pockets of voters in races that would be won on narrow margins. They were also strong believers in funding robust field programs and utilizing cutting-edge tactics to increase targeted voter turnout.

One of the things Parke and Steve strongly advocated for was to convert Asian American poll voters to absentee voters. This meant that instead of waiting for election day to turn out Chu's supporters, they could encourage these voters to get mail-in ballots and spend weeks chasing voters to drop the ballots in the mail early. This subtle tactic increased the likelihood of these voters to cast their ballots through convenience and time.

Anything can happen on election day to derail someone from voting. A sick child, waking up late, waking up with a hangover, a flat tire, being low on gas, needing an extra trip to the supermarket, or getting into an unexpected domestic argument could be just enough to prevent someone from going to the polls to vote. California voter turnout has broken all records since the state switched to all mail balloting, and various counties instituted early voting sites and ballot drop boxes. Giving a voter several weeks to drop off a ballot instead of just one day and what could be a long wait in line exponentially increases the likelihood of a voter to complete the task.

In addition to running an aggressive effort to convert Asian American poll voters to absentee voters, Parke and Steve created a broad tranche of Spanish and Chinese language mailers to supplement their typical mainstream English language program. Parke and Steve's strategic campaign innovations combined with Chu's aggressive field and fundraising operations greatly impacted the outcome of her dark horse race against a candidate strongly backed by California's formidable political establishment.

On election night, Chu took an early lead in absentee votes with 5,555 ballots. This was more than twice that of all other candidates combined. Chu won outright with 58% of the vote and had to be sworn into office in less than a week after the election in order to cast a critical vote to pass state legislation addressing California's electricity crisis caused by corporate market manipulations and capped retail electricity rates.

After the election, Chu was lauded for her efforts to bridge cultures and bring people together. The *Los Angeles Times* published a May 18, 2001 post-election report with the headline "Chu Is Known as a Bridge-Builder" and a July 1, 2001 article on Chu titled "Assemblywoman Praised for Reaching Across Ethnic Divide." Frank del Olmo, associate editor of the *Times*, wrote in an opinion piece published on May 20, 2001, "She turned ethnic politics on its head by reaching out to her Latino neighbors and convincing them she shared their views and aspirations."

Post-Election Impact

Once in office, Chu would go to work on increasing the representation of Asian Americans and giving them a stronger voice in the state's halls of power. She joined a single incumbent and two newly elected AAPI legislators (George Nakano, Wilma Chan, and Carol Liu) to form California's inaugural Asian American and Pacific Islander Legislative Caucus. Their work resulted in the establishment of the California Commission on Asian and Pacific Islander American Affairs.

As an Assemblymember, Chu was able to establish the Assembly Select Committee on Hate Crimes that convened statewide hearings to address the 9/11 racial backlash on Sikh and Muslim Americans

Chu garnered policy ideas from these hearings and authored landmark legislation that improved the prevention and prosecution of hate crimes. In addition, she overcame intense industry opposition to bills that would protect limited English-proficient AAPI consumers from predatory car sales practices and that increased the quality and broader acceptance of licensed acupuncturists as an effective alternative medical treatment.

When she was appointed to chair the Assembly Budget Subcommittee on Health and Human Services, she successfully fought to prevent devastating budget cuts to the state's most vulnerable populations.

A Voice for the Voiceless

Sometimes we think legislators only take on the big policy fights for large constituencies. Chu was different. She and her staff were deeply committed to giving a voice to AAPI immigrants who didn't speak English and didn't understand how to get help from the government.

Early into Chu's second term in office, a curious spectacle unfolded on a sidewalk adjacent to a car dealership in a city in her district.

A lone woman was wrapped in a sheet and marching back and forth on the sidewalk with a homemade sign that said "cheaters" on it. Coincidentally, a reporter for one of the Chinese print newspapers happened to be driving by and wondered what was going on. The reporter parked and went up to the protester and asked her why she was parading around wrapped in a bed sheet with a sign. The conversation unfolded in Chinese and the reporter discovered that the woman had been cheated by the car dealership and she was protesting on the sidewalk because she did not know what else she could do.

The reporter wrote a story in the Chinese paper about the woman's dilemma. The dealership marketed heavily to the Chinese-speaking community and she had visited it to buy a car. The salesperson negotiated a deal for a car with her in Chinese, but the contract she signed was in English. When she came to pick up the car, the car and financing terms were different from what she had negotiated. The dealership insisted that she had signed the contract and had no recourse but to accept the car and terms outlined in the contract. She was the victim of a bait-and-switch scheme that targeted and exploited non-English speaking Chinese.

The Asian Pacific American Legal Center of Southern California (APALC) read the story in the paper and decided to represent the woman and several other Chinese that they discovered had been similarly cheated. At the same time, APALC approached Chu to author a bill that would require contracts negotiated in Asian languages also be printed in the languages in which they were negotiated. Initially Chu and APALC demanded translation in all Asian languages and the bill faced intense opposition from the powerful banker, car dealership, automotive manufacturers, state chamber of commerce, business properties association, and financial services industries. In order to secure the votes needed for passage, Chu reduced the scope of the bill to require translations in only the largest Asian language groups (Chinese, Korean, Tagalog, and Vietnamese) and joined her bill to a Senate bill authored by the powerful chairwoman of the Senate Judiciary Committee, Martha Escutia, that also dealt with translations of contracts.

Despite unabated industry opposition to Chu's bill, AB 309 was signed into law by the governor and helped pressure the dealership at fault to settle the lawsuit brought by APALC on behalf of the Chinese immigrants.

Several months after the bill was signed into law, the *Los Angeles Times* reported, "The plaintiffs who filed the lawsuit against Wondries in 2002 announced Tuesday that they had settled with the car dealership and received an undisclosed financial sum and letters of apology. The settlement comes two and a half months before the full implementation of a state law that will require certain business contracts to be written in four major Asian languages—Chinese, Korean, Tagalog and Vietnamese—when needed. Consumer advocates hope the law, whose impetus was the Wondries case, will allow consumers to rely on documents, rather than off-the-cuff translations by salesclerks."

Budget Fight

In one legislative gambit, Chu blocked cuts to a program that provided access to clinic services for nearly 300,000 low-income single mothers. The proposed cut was diabolically complex. It was like the board game Mousetrap where a wildly arcane set of policy changes interacted with each other, resulting in the disqualification of low-income single mothers from the state-supported health care services.

Diane Van Maren, the health policy budget consultant for the state Senate, whom I worked with under Hilda Solis, alerted me to the problem in the budget and I relayed it to Assemblywoman Chu. Once Chu understood what was at stake, she defied legislative leaders and held up the budget until this issue was resolved. The passage of the state budget that year literally rested on addressing

Chu's refusal to capitulate on this issue. But she didn't just oppose the cut; she had a plan to recalculate costs to balance the budget and give these women the opportunity to requalify for support if they were inadvertently dropped from the program. She was called in to meet with Speaker Herb Wesson and his top budget aide to resolve the impasse. After Chu walked them through her novel solution to the problem, they agreed to her proposal and the long state budget stalemate ended within days.

The most dramatic action Chu took while chair of the Budget Subcommittee on Health and Human Services was fighting to block massive cuts to state Medicaid funding for the disabled. Facing a potential budget shortfall of billions, some Democratic leaders pushed for quick cuts to show the public that the Democratic Party was acting responsibly to meet the crisis and keep the state solvent.

Blocking the cuts would not be easy. The public didn't understand the ramifications of the state budget cuts, and Democratic efforts to explain them were completely incomprehensible.

On its face, the cuts seemed sensible. The proposed reductions were directed at what was called "Medi-Cal Optional Benefits." Medi-Cal is California's Medicaid healthcare program. Medicaid is the joint federal and state program that covers some medical costs for certain people with limited income and resources.

What would be more sensible than to cut "optional" funding for a program? Well, in this case the word "optional" meant that it was "optional" for the state to fund the program, not that the types of benefits involved were "optional" for the patients who needed them.

These "optional" benefits covered wheelchairs, prosthetics, catheters, and colostomy bags for low-income disabled individuals. Once Chu made this clear to her Democratic colleagues, support for the cuts faltered within the Caucus. While she won the debate within the Caucus, she knew she still needed to be able to make the case for rejecting cuts to the voters of California.

This is where she ran into the typical suboptimal messaging used by Democrats. Somewhere along the way in California's budget process the term "budget cuts" morphed into "budget savings." Perhaps someone in the communications shop thought that voters would be less angry at Democrats for voting for "savings" than "cuts."

Chu had a different perspective.

First, she believed it was unconscionable for Democrats to vote in support of the budget cuts to the most vulnerable regardless of the political ramifications. Second, she believed that base Democratic voters would rally behind Assembly Democrats if the caucus took a bold stand against the cuts. She pushed legislative leaders to allow her to hold a public hearing on the proposed cuts. Initially they were reluctant to approve a hearing and thought it would expose the Democratic Caucus to criticism if the cuts were inevitable. Leadership reasoned that a public hearing would only amplify the devastating impact of cuts they thought Democrats would ultimately have no choice but to make. Chu persisted and ultimately won the approval of leaders once she outlined her plan for the hearing and how it could rally Californians behind the Democrats.

The first challenge Chu faced was how the legislature organized and presented budget hearings. Traditionally, budget hearing agendas were organized in order of obscure budget item numbers and vague technical names and acronyms for programmatic areas or services (such as "Medi-Cal Optional Services"). Staff is trained to write analyses of the programs to be funded or cut for legislators and civil service staff who know what the terms and item numbers mean. For the general public, the terminology is ambiguous or completely opaque.

Chu proposed a radical change to standard fiscal committee practice of using these vague terms and item numbers. Instead of issuing a public agenda of proposed cuts that referred only to item numbers and technical terms, she demanded that the agenda be organized by the plain description of the groups that would be impacted by the cuts. She knew that referring to populations and programs only by item numbers dehumanized the cuts and obscured the true impact from the state's voters. Chu got her way and the committee agenda that was available to the public listed the following panels:

Panel 1: Adults, Elderly & Disabled

Panel 2: Children and Families

Panel 3: Impact of Medi-Cal Cuts on Patient Care

The second challenge was to overcome the standard legislative practice of convening hearings in venues least accessible to the public and media. The state capitol is the venue preferred by staff and legislators. However, the ancient capitol building where hearings are usually held is also difficult to navigate and not easily accessible to the disabled. To increase the reach of the hearing, Chu proposed convening it in downtown Los Angeles at a modern state building where it would be more accessible to the disabled and other populations affected by the cuts and provide an opportunity for the conversation on budget cuts to be covered by the press in the largest media market in the state.

Chu also instructed staff and advocates to organize affected constituencies to show up for the hearings. On the day of the hearing, the venue was packed. The line of people assembled to attend and testify was truly impressive. Over 400 people attended the weekday hearing. Equally impressive was the gaggle of reporters and television cameras assembled to cover the hearing. The entire front row was reserved for individuals in wheelchairs and their attendant caregivers. Chu reasoned that if lawmakers at the hearing intended to demand budget cuts in health and human services, they would have had to do it while looking into the eyes of those most affected.

During the hearing Chu went even a step further. As she was

explaining to the audience what the proposed cuts were, she hoisted a catheter and colostomy bag in her grip high enough for the audience (and press) to see what would be cut. The dramatic move resulted in some audible gasps from the audience.

Chu was not going to back down, and she used this hearing to go all in to shift public opinion on budget cuts. Originally, the public sentiment was that the state deficit was a product of irresponsible spending on liberal giveaways to freeloaders. This hearing gave a human face to the reality of the cuts and helped mobilize public support for alternative approaches to balance the state budget. The pressure forced legislators to work harder to find additional revenue to cover the deficit and take cuts in areas that did not have the same life-or-death consequences as was previously proposed. Without a doubt, Chu's heroics and relentless efforts were the key to sparing "Medi-Cal Optional Benefits" from being eliminated in the budget.

In recognition of her legislative skill, fiscal expertise, and reliability on progressive issues, Chu was subsequently chosen to chair the Assembly Appropriations Committee. It is considered the most powerful committee in the Assembly because it has jurisdiction over every bill that involves any form of state funding. Not only would the chair have incredible influence over policy originating in the Assembly, it would also allow the chair to influence Senate bills that were destined to be considered by the committee on their way to the Assembly Floor and eventually the governor's office.

Chu was the first Asian American to chair the most powerful committee in the Assembly. This was quite a feat considering that she entered the Assembly in 2001 with no legislation and no standing committee chairmanship, and was assigned to the smallest office in the building that is affectionately known today as "The Dog House." As chair of the Assembly Appropriations Committee and therefore a member of the Joint Budget Conference Committee charged with reconciling the annual state budget, Chu fought for low-wage workers and continued to protect the state's safety net from crippling cuts as multibillion-dollar budget deficits continued to vex the legislature.

Farmworker Heat Safety

It was not unusual for Chu to swing for the fences on issues that were important to her. As a legislator, she was one of labor's strongest advocates. She also preferred hiring organizers for staff instead of insular policy wonks from elite colleges. So when one of her staff, a former United Farm Workers (UFW) union organizer named Merlyn Calderon, came to her to author a bill sponsored by California Rural Legal Assistance to require farms to provide workers with protective shade and hydration for farm workers, Chu chose to lean in and pick a fight with Big Ag.

It was unusual for an urban legislator to take on a rural issue like heat protection for farm workers, but Chu was sympathetic on the issue because of her history supporting farm workers and her large Latino constituency. More importantly, she and the sponsors of the bill knew that her position as Appropriations Committee chair would give this bill added leverage that an average legislator could not.

At the time, a deadly heat wave was killing farm workers in the fields regularly. Articles in major newspapers reported the deaths and editorialized on the urgency to pass a law forcing farmers to provide shade and water breaks to stem the tide of heat-related deaths. To emphasize the intensity of the situation, State Senator Dean Flores organized a high noon hearing on the topic in the middle of an open farm field in Shafter.

Legislators, including Chu, made the long journey to this field in the middle of nowhere to hear directly from farm workers and experience the deadly heat that the workers toiled in on a daily basis. There was no shade. Senator Flores was a master in the lost art of political staging. He staged a group of trucks backed into a rough semicircle. Legislators and representatives from the governor's office sat in the blistering heat on the lowered tailgates of these trucks in a makeshift forum in the fields as farm workers told their stories of the sweltering working conditions they had to endure. Chu had brought a large, round weather thermometer to the gathering to show reporters how hot it got. At one point, the thermometer read 115 degrees Fahrenheit.

Chu aggressively pressed the legislation forward and the press continued to highlight the growing farm worker body count and the impact on the families left behind. Senator Flores worked feverishly behind the scenes to negotiate a deal with Governor Schwarzenegger to address the crisis. As legislative deadlines loomed and time was running out, the governor agreed to put regulations in place to provide shade and water breaks for farm workers on the condition that Chu drop her bill. Lesser legislators would have let ego carry the day and refuse, but Chu took the path to serve the greater good and relented to shelving her bill with the guarantee that farm workers would receive some relief sooner rather than later.

Tax Amnesty

One of her greatest achievements as Appropriations chair was the passage of her proposal to extend a state tax amnesty in an attempt to collect hundreds of millions of dollars in late and underpaid taxes. Instead of raising taxes during difficult economic times, Chu reasoned that some or all of the proposed budget cuts to safety net programs could be avoided by doing a better job collecting the taxes that were already owed to the state but went unpaid.

Chu was able to use her position as Appropriations chair to force the inclusion of the tax amnesty language in her bill into the state budget. The Assembly Appropriations Committee's tax policy expert, Steve Shea, and Chu's senior legislative aide, Julio Martinez, played a critical role in crafting the language and staffing her innovative revenue proposal.

The effort was a massive success. Government analysts initially estimated that the tax amnesty would only bring in a few hundred million. After passage and implementation of the amnesty, preliminary tax recoveries helped to protect some key safety-net programs from severe cuts. By February of the following year of its implementation, the state's tax agency had collected $1.4 *billion* and had helped California avert an unprecedented budget disaster.

AAPI Representation

With regard to protecting AAPI representation, Chu's election victory would be critical to ensuring fair representation for AAPIs in Los Angeles County's San Gabriel Valley. In 2001, state redistricting was still controlled by the legislature and the process favored incumbents. Had she not won, the AAPIs in the San Gabriel Valley could have easily been divided into separate districts in order to dilute their vote and prevent them from ever electing an AAPI representative again.

Chu's victory allowed her to have a strong voice in the final maps. She demonstrated her resolve as an AAPI woman and exercised her power as an incumbent when a group of male legislators made a late-night attempt to corner her in a nearly deserted office building across from the Capitol with the intent of intimidating her into ceding key segments of the district in order to significantly weaken the AAPI vote. Chu defied them and courageously held her ground, figuratively and literally, against the heavy-handed effort to weaken the voting power of AAPI communities in the San Gabriel Valley.

As a result, AAPI voters the 49th Assembly district were kept together and the district has been represented by an AAPI in the Assembly for over two decades since Chu's election in 2001. It is now considered an AAPI district. After being termed out of the Assembly and serving as chair of the California State Board of Equalization, Chu would go on to represent significant AAPI portions of the district as a member of the United States House of Representatives from 2009 to the present.

In addition to serving the constituents of the 49th Assembly District, Chu took on a broader role in empowering AAPIs throughout the state. During her time as Appropriations Committee chair, she also chaired the California Asian and Pacific Islander American Legislative Caucus. She used this position to conceive and convene an annual statewide summit of AAPI advocacy groups in order to increase the community's voice in budget and policy decisions made in Sacramento.

She also led efforts to advance AAPIs in elected office. She actively supported numerous AAPIs running for local, state, and federal office. Her support significantly helped Betty Yee secure a seat on the state Board of Equalization and to elect Ted Lieu to the state Assembly. Lieu used the Assembly as a launching pad for a successful political career that included service in the state Senate and led to his eventual election to the United States House of Representatives. Today, Lieu is the House Democratic Caucus Vice Chair and the highest-ranking Asian American in the history of congressional Democratic House leadership.

Lastly, Chu was a champion of building a diverse staff pipeline. She believed that AAPI elected officials need a reliable pipeline of staff at all levels in order to best accomplish the tasks necessary to ensure proper AAPI representation in the halls of power. At the time, Latino and Black legislators made it a top priority to encourage opportunities for Latino and Black staff knowing that institutional barriers prevented many people of color from gaining the experience and training necessary for career advancement. Opportunities for AAPI staff to work in the capitol were even more scarce. As an assemblywoman, Chu made it a point to recruit, train, and nurture qualified but underrepresented AAPI staff. As a result, her office produced young staff standouts like Angela Pan, Annie Lam, Andrew Medina, Natalie Chu, Pearl Fu, Ricky Choi, Liz Lee, Susan Hsieh, and Gloria Lin. They would all lead successful careers in public service, nonprofits, and the private sector. Angela Pan went on to serve in the United States Foreign Service as a member of the elite corps of advance staff for U.S. Secretary of State Hillary Clinton and Annie Lam became a successful founder of several nonprofit organizations dedicated to growing the pipeline of AAPI elected officials and training career government staff. Chu also recruited and nurtured all-star Latino staff such as Julio Martinez who went on to become chief of staff to Assemblyman Mike Eng, Merlyn Calderon who went on to serve in the United States Foreign Service, Alejandra Sotelo-Solis who went on to serve as mayor of National City, and Cristal Wallin who went on to serve as Director of Administration & Strategic Planning, Administration and Finance at San Francisco State University. Chu would carry on the mission of providing opportunities for a legion of AAPI staff to serve at the Board of Equalization and in the U.S. Congress. In Congress, three successive AAPI women served as Chu's chiefs of staff: Amelia Wang, Linda Shim, and Sonali Desai.

CHAPTER 4

2006 Board of Equalization Campaign

"So in war, the way is to avoid what is strong, and strike at what is weak."
—SUN TZU

Facing the term limit of her service in the Assembly in 2006, Judy Chu made the decision in 2005 to run for the state Board of Equalization seat held by John Chiang, who was also termed out and running for state controller. Four of the five members of the Board are elected by voters in massive districts with millions of voters in each. These four members are state constitutional officers. The fifth seat on the Board is held by the state controller. The Board seat Chu would be vying for was the densest and most compact out of the four districts. It comprised the entirety of Los Angeles County and leaned heavily in favor of Democratic candidates. As such, the winner of the Democratic primary election would be the presumptive victor in the general election.

This race would not be an easy one. Chu's Democratic primary election opponent was fellow state Assemblymember Jerome Horton. He was chair of the Assembly's powerful Governmental Organization Committee that had jurisdiction over gaming, tobacco, and alcohol policy. It was one of the Assembly's "juice" committees, meaning that it had a lot of power and allowed its chair to raise outrageous sums of campaign money. Horton had been eyeing this seat for a long time.

His campaign war chest at the time eclipsed Chu's and he had over a year head start on getting key endorsements, including that of the current speaker of the Assembly.

Horton was a tenacious competitor with deep political ties in Los Angeles County. He was also considered a "Mod" (moderate Democrat). His votes usually favored business interests, but he was a savvy strategist and kept many of his votes in line with organized labor enough to maintain their powerful support. By threading the needle between business and labor, Horton was able to raise funds from both sides and was the presumptive frontrunner in this race.

While Chu was considered the underdog in this race, she had a few factors in her favor. Despite being behind Horton in cash on hand, Chu was an incredible fundraiser and could conceivably close the money gap. Chu still lagged behind Horton in endorsements, but many of the endorsements Horton had would not have a significant impact on voter decisions in Los Angeles County. Chu still had the chance to secure what would be the most important endorsements in this race. In order to pull out a win in this dark horse campaign, Chu would have to run a flawless campaign and employ a tactic made famous by the ancient Spartans.

In 480 BCE, 300 Spartans and soldiers from the Greek alliance for a total force of approximately 7,000 chose to battle invading Persians at Thermopylae, which was directly on the path into Greece. The narrow pass of Thermopylae is believed to have been under 400 meters wide and created a bottleneck that eliminated the Persian army's numerical superiority. Using this force multiplier tactic, the small Spartan and Greek Alliance successfully held off what was estimated to be 120,000 to 200,000 Persian soldiers at the Battle of Thermopylae.

In order to win the Board of Equalization seat, Chu would have to find a political battleground where she could reduce Horton's campaign cash and endorsement advantage.

Chu's consultants, Parke Skelton and Steve Barkan, determined that the fight for the Democratic Party endorsement could be Chu's Thermopylae. In contested partisan primary elections, political party endorsements can have tremendous impact. Voters view the endorsement as a key factor in deciding who to vote for in a primary election. In addition, the winner of the endorsement is included on the Democratic Party's slate mailer that is sent to nearly every registered Democratic voter in the state. That's millions of pieces of free campaign mail for the endorsed candidate. Most of the time, candidates vying for the endorsement go only as far as hosting elaborate cocktail parties at the endorsing convention and mailing a few flyers to delegates. At best, these candidates would only spend a few thousand dollars on courting delegate support to win the party endorsement.

On the advice of Skelton and Barkan, Chu would go all in on getting the California Democratic Party endorsement. Instead of spending precious campaign cash in a futile attempt to reach millions of voters in the primary election, Chu would spend tens of thousands of dollars reaching out to approximately 3,000 Democratic Party delegates. The campaign designed by Barkan included nightly phone banks where volunteers would make calls to delegates and if they got a live one on the line they would hand the phone to Chu, who could make a direct personal appeal for support. This happened almost every evening for weeks running up to the state convention. In addition, Barkan designed ingeniously micro-targeted letters matching Chu's key regional statewide endorsements with individual delegates in those same regions. To save money, these mailers were assembled at my house after work by me and my wife Sylvia along with a small volunteer army of young and enthusiastic AAPI legislative staffers.

The strategy allowed Chu to force Horton to battle her in terrain that favored her profile over his. Horton was a Democrat, but known as a pro-business wheeler-dealer who called himself "Mr. 41" because he would jockey to be the deciding vote on controversial bills that favored the business over workers or the environment. At the time, Democratic Party delegates frowned upon moderate Democratic politicians. This provided the perfect juxtaposition to Horton that Chu would lean into.

Chu's team produced round blue stickers that had the slogan "True Blue Judy Chu." The slogan stuck and boosted her Democratic Party campaign that contrasted her rock-solid progressive bona fides against Horton's moderate pro-business leanings. She also positioned herself as the Democratic stalwart fighting Republican Governor Arnold Schwarzenegger. In a speech to Democratic delegates, she proclaimed that Governor Schwarzenegger's budget cuts amounted to a war on Californians and that she declared war on him. Chu also hosted a true blue-themed hospitality suite titled "Ice Cream for Change" for party delegates that featured bags of blue jelly beans and an inflatable punching bag with Governor Schwarzenegger's face on it. The delegates loved it and lined up to give the governor a punch in the face before getting a liberal scoop of ice cream.

The bold play worked. Chu won 65.2% of the delegate vote and secured the pivotal Democratic Party endorsement. The Democratic Party's slate mailer touting Chu as the Democratic Party endorsed candidate mailed to millions of Democratic voters in Los Angeles County, along with Barkan's innovative cost-cutting printing strategies and tightly targeted direct mail, helped Chu match Horton almost dollar for dollar on voter contact. Chu's unparalleled record of responsible fiscal stewardship in the course of balancing the state budget and passing the landmark tax amnesty proposal helped her earn key Southern California newspaper endorsements. Moreover, the free positive press further cut into Horton's paid media advantage. Combined, all these elements produced a primary election night victory for Chu that would also guarantee her a win in November.

CHAPTER 5

2009 Congressional Campaign

"Appear weak when you are strong, and strong when you are weak."

—SUN TZU

In February 2009, President Barack Obama appointed U.S. Representative Hilda L. Solis to U.S. Secretary of Labor and precipitated a special election for her seat that encompassed Los Angeles' San Gabriel suburbs. This was Chu's backyard and it would be an unprecedented opportunity for her to serve in Congress. The seat was still heavily populated by Latinos and would attract strong Latino candidates that considered this a "Latino seat." As a presidential appointee, Solis would not be able to openly support Chu as she had done in the past. Nevertheless, Chu hoped that she could win the seat with the support of a coalition of labor leaders and elected officials that were part of Solis' political machinery along with the support of the contingent of Latino local elected officials with whom Chu had diligently worked with directly to build strong alliances.

State Senator Gil Cedillo, a popular elected official among activist Latinos, filed to run for the Solis seat. As a former state assemblymember and sitting state senator, Cedillo had deep political ties that could help him amass a formidable war chest and secure key endorsements. He was well known for his relentless efforts to pass a law that would allow undocumented immigrants to obtain state driver's licenses. As a former labor leader, gifted orator, and wily political tactician, he would be a formidable opponent. He would also be backed by the Latino Legislative Caucus and the Congressional Hispanic Caucus, both powerful political entities.

Chu would not have this same advantage. The Asian American and Pacific Islander Legislative Caucus and the Congressional Asian Pacific American Caucus were both much smaller and only in their infancies at the time. They had fewer resources and political experience to offer Chu. Fortunately, Chu's many competitive races over the preceding decades provided a small but battle-tested army of volunteers and an impressive base of AAPI donors that would help her raise the funds necessary to run a competitive congressional campaign.

Chu faced perhaps her toughest race to date against Cedillo. Never before had the stakes been this high. A seat in Congress is highly coveted and considered among the most prestigious in the world. This would be a battle that would go to the bitter end. Cedillo and his backers would go to any length to win, and Chu would have to fight for every advantage she could get if she would have any chance of winning this seat.

Winning the Democratic Party endorsement had been pivotal for Chu in 2001 and 2006 and it would be again in the 2009 special election. However, this time the tactic would have an unexpected twist. As Chu secured pledges of support from delegates, Cedillo countered with nearly an equal number of delegates. At the time, other sitting legislators, congressional members, and constitutional officers had the power to appoint a small number of delegates and could also temporarily swap them with delegates who lived in the district of candidates who were seeking the party endorsement. Both Chu and Cedillo employed this method to alter the odds in their favor for the party endorsement. Both would fight to a draw in the early stages of the process. While Chu had the better organizing machine, Cedillo only needed to secure enough delegates to prevent Chu from reaching the requisite super-majority vote threshold to win the endorsement. As the deadline to swap delegates approached, it appeared that Cedillo had enough support to block Chu from winning the endorsement.

However, Chu would play an ace in the hole that Cedillo did not anticipate.

Democratic Party rules at the time allowed Democratic candidates known as "Great Americans" that ran as Democrats in safe Republican districts to have two delegate appointments. They were called "Great Americans" because they ran in districts that were impossible for a Democrat to win in. The Democratic Party valued them because their candidacy would help to irritate Republican candidates, help drive statewide Democratic turnout, and force the Republican Party to spend money in safe red districts. As valiant as these candidates were, they were also typically treated by the Democratic legislative establishment as afterthoughts. Basically, few if any legislators ever gave these people the time of day despite their devoted service to the Party.

Chu understood their power and personally reached out to them for their support. Many of them were true believers in the Democratic Party, and Chu's progressive credentials appealed strongly to them. It was also the first and only time many of them would be courted by a state constitutional officer. By treating these Great Americans as important players in the Democratic Party, Chu was able to win the support of an overwhelming number of them. By the time Cedillo realized what the Chu campaign was doing, it was too late and the vast majority of Great Americans had already released their delegate spots to Chu.

When the deadline to submit delegate changes came and went, it was clear that Chu had more than enough votes to win the endorsement. So much so that Cedillo and his supporters didn't even show up to the endorsement meeting to vote. Chu's gambit was so effective and controversial that the state Democratic Party would change its rules to prevent future campaigns from running the same play.

The highly contentious campaign played out as expected. Both campaigns threw everything including the kitchen sink into the fight. The Solis coalition's support and the Democratic Party endorsement did play an outsized role in the race, and Chu would go on to beat Cedillo and six other Democrats in the special election primary.

In a bizarre twist of fate and possibly an intentional attempt to confuse voters, Judy Chu would go on from the primary victory over Cedillo to face her Republican cousin-in-law, Betty Tom Chu. The *San Gabriel Valley Tribune* commented, "Chu and Chu are known to be political rivals, and some wonder if the Betty Tom Chu's entrance is an effort to cause confusion." Betty had been mayor of Monterey Park and was well-known locally as the first Chinese American woman to pass the California State Bar Exam. While the district heavily favored Democrats, Team Judy Chu was concerned that two candidates sharing the same surname on the ballot would confuse voters…especially Chinese American voters. In a low-turnout special election scenario involving less informed voters, Judy Chu could not count on the typical partisan outcome that would favor a Democrat. This meant that despite surviving a grueling primary election fight with Cedillo, Judy Chu would have to retrench and mount another all-out campaign in what would have otherwise been an easy runoff.

Clark Lee was running Judy Chu's AAPI voter contact program. He was fluent in Chinese and an expert on field campaign management and AAPI voter outreach programs. He would later become the political director for the California Democratic Party and founded his own campaign consulting firm, Thinking Cap Strategies. He recommended that Chinese voter messaging focus on the Chinese character in Judy's given name that differentiated her from Betty. Judy's Chinese given name was 美心 and Betty's was 美生. The distinguishing character in Judy's name was 心, which translates to "heart." The character was emphasized in all Chinese language voter communication, and heart-shaped (♡) graphics were integrated into mail pieces. The tactic worked and Judy went on to beat Betty 63% to 33% in the July runoff.

Post-Election Impact

Chu was called to Washington immediately after the runoff to be sworn in so that she could cast critical House votes in support of the President Obama's landmark Affordable Care Act proposal. Chu became the first Chinese American woman elected to serve in the U.S. House of Representatives when she was sworn in by House Speaker Nancy Pelosi on July 14, 2009.

As a member of Congress, Chu has led the national fight to author and pass the Women's Health Protection Act to guarantee access to safe and legal abortions. She gained national attention carrying the bill in the aftermath of the U.S. Supreme Court's reversal of *Roe v. Wade* in the Dobbs decision. Representative Chu currently serves on the powerful House Ways and Means Committee, which has jurisdiction over legislation pertaining to taxes, revenues, Social Security, and Medicare. In that Committee, Representative Chu is a member of the Subcommittees on Health, giving her oversight over healthcare reform and crucial safety net programs, Worker and Family Support, and Oversight.

Chu also founded and co-chairs the Congressional Creative Rights Caucus, which advocates for the copyright protections of those in the creative industries, such as music, film, and visual arts. Chu's other accomplishments in Congress include: introducing and passing a Congressional resolution of regret for the

Chinese Exclusion Act of 1882, working with President Obama to declare the San Gabriel Mountains a national monument, and requiring the Department of Defense to address military hazing. Chu was elected chair of the Congressional Asian Pacific American Caucus (CAPAC) in 2011. Since taking the helm, the number of AAPIs serving in Congress has grown to 21. CAPAC actively supported the election of President Joe Biden and Vice President Kamala Harris (who is of South Asian descent) in 2020 as well as key U.S. Senate races in swing states with significant AAPI populations. CAPAC's tireless advocacy internally to the Democratic Party apparatus to reach out to AAPI voters delivered victories for Democrats in places like Georgia, Nevada, and Pennsylvania. The growth of CAPAC's influence has led to an exponential increase in power and influence of AAPIs on high-level appointments and national policy. Due in large part to Chu and CAPAC, AAPIs became the margin of victory on Election Day and now have a seat at the table.

CAPAC's push for more AAPI representation in the Biden Administration produced the following appointments: Katherine Tai as the 19th U.S. Trade Representative (a position with the rank of ambassador and a cabinet-level post), Julie Su as U.S. deputy secretary of labor, Arati Prabhakar as director of the White House Office of Science and Technology Policy (a cabinet-level post) and science advisor to the president, Rohit Chopra as director of the Consumer Financial Protection Bureau, and Erika Moritsugu as deputy assistant to the president and Asian American and Pacific Islander senior liaison.

In response to the epidemic of AAPI hate spread by Republican promotion of terms like "China virus" and "Kung Flu," CAPAC passed the COVID-19 Hate Crimes Act and the bill to start the process of establishing a national Smithsonian museum of AAPI history. Both were signed into law by President Biden while CAPAC members stood at his side in the White House. CAPAC also successfully worked to remove anti-Asian provisions in the Creating Helpful Incentives to Produce Semiconductors (CHIPS) and Science Act of 2022 to ensure that improving the nation's competitiveness would not come at the expense of AAPI civil rights.

Another sign of the growing political power and influence of AAPIs in Congress is the election of CAPAC member U.S. Representative Ted Lieu as the House Democratic Caucus vice chair in 2022. Lieu beat out three other candidates to win the fifth-highest ranking post in House Democratic Leadership. He is the highest-ranking AAPI in House Democratic Leadership history. CAPAC Chair Chu also holds a position in House Democratic Leadership as a member of the Steering and Policy Committee.

PART III

The Margin of Victory

"To go wrong in one's own way is better than to go right in someone else's."

— FYODOR DOSTOEVSKY

This section of the book is about some of the other political fights I've been involved in. These fights were as much about defending as they were about defining our place as AAPIs in modern American politics.

The condescending dismissal of AAPI voter power and characterization of us as exotic oddities and political afterthoughts was a regular occurrence along my 30-year political journey. What was worse was that some Asian Americans went along with these myths.

I would burn with rage when I experienced this condescension. That anger would smolder within me for decades. So much so that it drove me to take on any fight that would give me the opportunity to prove naysayers wrong and chip away at tired tropes of Asian Americans as politically insignificant or irrelevant.

Here are some stories of the fights that helped to redefine us and demonstrated the emergent political power of AAPI communities.

CHAPTER 6

The Asian American Small Business PAC

"If you want to go fast, go alone. If you want to go far, go together."
—AFRICAN PROVERB

As the number of AAPI elected officials began to grow in California in the 2000s, it became clear to Asian American leaders that the growth would be unsustainable without building the political infrastructure necessary to support viable but under-resourced AAPI candidates. Prior to this revelation, AAPI candidates were left to fend for themselves in campaign fundraising and voter contact.

Other communities had developed deep benches of candidates, established a farm program for campaign operatives, and leveraged elected office to drive support for aligned political action committees (PAC) that could support candidates with direct donations and unlimited independent expenditures campaigns. Political action committees have no spending limits when they independently support candidates with mail, television, or digital advertisements, or voter contact in the field as long as there is no direct coordination with the candidate that the PAC is supporting.

In 2005, a trio of influential individuals took it upon themselves to assemble the resources necessary to elect an unprecedented number of AAPIs to state legislative and constitutional offices in 2006 with the intent to someday position one of them as a viable candidate for the governorship of California. Jadine Chin Nielsen, Lucy McCoy, and James Santa Maria established the Asian American Small Business Political Action Committee in June 2005. The three were seasoned political insiders who cut their teeth as top lieutenants in heavyweight political circles.

Jadine began her career with U.S. Senator Alan Cranston, serving as his California state director, and managed the senator's political and public policy initiatives. After Cranston, she was the campaign manager for Mayor Richard Riordan in Los Angeles, Northern California campaign manager for the Clinton for President primary campaign, California Director of Scheduling and Advance for the Clinton-Gore campaign, and political consultant to Kathleen Connell and Jane Harman in their campaigns for state controller and the U.S. House of Representatives, respectively. In Hawaii, she served as senior advisor to Mazie Hirono's gubernatorial and Congressional campaigns, state director for the Edwards for President primary campaign, and Democratic National Committee state director for the Kerry-Edwards presidential campaign.

In between political campaigns, she took high-level roles inside the government. She became the first Asian American to serve as the deputy mayor for the City of Los Angeles, joined the Clinton Administration where she served in the White House as presidential transition search manager at the Office of Presidential Personnel, was appointed chief of staff at the U.S. Small Business Administration, and subsequently was appointed as deputy to the chairman of the Federal Deposit Insurance Corporation (FDIC). Jadine chaired both the Asian American Small Business Political Action Committee in California and the Patsy T. Mink Political Action Committee in Hawaii. To this day, she continues to be a respected Democratic powerbroker and master consigliere to the political elite on the Hawaiian islands.

Jadine's close friend and partner in politics is Lucy McCoy. Lucy's political reach is impressive. She founded a Los Angeles-based firm that provided public affairs advocacy services, managed local initiative campaigns, and provided fundraising services for political campaigns and nonprofit entities. Lucy was tapped to lead the high-profile effort to bring the 2000 Democratic National Convention to the City of Los Angeles and served as president of the Los Angeles 2000 DNC Host Committee.

Lucy was a leader in numerous civic and community-based organizations. Among these, she served on the U.S. Small Business Administration's National Advisory Committee, Board of Trustees and Executive Committee of the Board of Brentwood School, the Executive Committee of the California Breast Cancer Research Program, and the Foundation Board of the California Science Center, and was a Board co-founder and Executive Committee member of the Beyond Differences Foundation. She was also a member of the Executive Committee and Board of the Los Angeles Business Council. More importantly, Lucy mentored a generation of political operatives that now populate the halls of power in the city and county of Los Angeles. One such operative is James Santa Maria.

Both Jadine and Lucy were a big part of James Santa Maria's political rise as a city hall insider and Southern California power player. His early experience included serving as staff in Jadine's deputy mayor office inside Richard Riordan's mayoral administration. He would go on to serve as deputy chief of staff to Los Angeles City Councilmember Rudy Svorinich, Jr. and chief of staff to Los Angeles City Councilmember Nick Pacheco before starting his own firm, the Santa Maria Group, a leading government relations, public affairs, and political campaigns consulting firm.

James uses his insider knowledge and political reach to help communities and companies successfully navigate the halls of government. He also spends much of his time mentoring young AAPI staff and political professionals in the same way Jadine and Lucy mentored him. He has utilized his influence to support a vast throng of AAPI candidates and numerous AAPI non-profit organizations. Whenever I visited James at his downtown Los Angeles office, I would invariably see a parade of the region's who's who list of political players sauntering in and out of his suite like it was their second home. Whether it was for powerful local interests or the Asian American community, James was an all-in type of political player who was never shy about throwing sharp elbows or leaning into wayward politicians when necessary.

In 2006, the Asian American Small Business PAC raised nearly $300,000 with the help of the California Asian American and Pacific Islander Legislative Caucus Chairman Alberto Torrico to support a historic number of AAPI candidates running for office. In the primary election, AASB PAC hired Ron Wong and Imprenta Communications to develop and execute an independent expenditure effort that included 100,000 direct mail units, 30,000 GOTV live calls, and 90,000 GOTV emails. The direct mail employed an innovative slate format allowing multiple Asian American candidates to be served by a single piece of mail. For example, mailers to voters supporting Mike Eng for state Assembly in the 49th District based in Los Angeles County's San Gabriel Valley included appeals to support John Chiang, who was running statewide, and Judy Chu, who was running for the Board of Equalization seat, also based in Los Angeles County. This allowed the PAC to triple up on each mailer and cut costs without weakening voter contact. In the general election, AASB donated $45,000 to a labor-run independent expenditure effort that helped John Chiang overcome a last-minute, multimillion-dollar special interest attack. With the help of the Asian American Small Business PAC, Mike Eng, Judy Chu, and John Chiang all won highly competitive campaigns against well-funded opponents.

AASB PAC's efforts would be the first time in state history that a political action committee run by experienced Asian American political operatives raised funds at scale and utilized an award-winning Asian American-owned political consulting firm, Imprenta Communications, to successfully elect Asian American candidates with direct campaign contributions and independent expenditures sustained over a period of twelve years.

I served as the political director for the PAC from 2007 to 2013 and between 2014 and mid 2017. In 2007-2008, AASB was the second largest contributor to an independent expenditure effort that included a field outreach effort that touched 100,000 households, 30,000 calls, and 75,000 direct mail units to help Warren Furutani win the special election in the 55th Assembly District. In 2008, AASB funded a surgically targeted independent expenditure effort in support of Paul Fong for the 22nd Assembly District and helped him narrowly overcome an opponent that outspent Fong two-to-one during the campaign.

Over the course of ten of its twelve years of existence, I led AASB PAC's efforts to raise over $2 million, support 52 AAPI candidates, and win 65% of the AAPI races it participated in. The PAC had substantially contributed to the astronomical rise of AAPI representatives in the halls of state and local government and supported John Chiang's steady journey from State Board of Equalization member to state controller, state treasurer, and finally contender for governor for California. Overall, the Asian American Small Business PAC made direct contributions and independent expenditures of nearly $300,000 in support of Chiang's various election efforts.

Jadine, Lucy, and James were completely fearless with the PAC. They made many tough decisions. The trio never shied away from a fight and took the brunt of many disgruntled high-ranking legislators and powerful special interest groups. Watching them operate and being able to work with them was an education and privilege of a lifetime. When I had to make tough calls, these three stood by me undauntedly.

The AASB PAC was ultimately retired in 2019 after establishing an unparalleled record of successfully electing AAPIs to local, state, and federal office throughout the nation.

CHAPTER 7

Million More Voters

"Individually, we are one drop. Together, we are an ocean."

—RYUNOSUKE SATORO

California's 2010 gubernatorial race would be a turning point for AAPI political power. Prior to 2010, convincing mainstream campaigns to invest in courting and turning out AAPI at scale was an impossible task. Mainstream consultants would say that AAPIs don't vote or were too hard to communicate with because of the multitudes of AAPI languages spoken.

The race for the golden state's governorship pitted former Democratic governor Jerry Brown against Republican tech entrepreneur Meg Whitman. When Jerry Brown last served in Sacramento from 1975 to 1983, he pursued a visionary agenda that was perceived by the public as eccentric and inspired *Chicago Times* columnist Mike Royko to describe him as "Governor Moonbeam." Brown would become much less controversial between 1983 and 2010, but political insiders still feared that Whitman's massive wealth and reputation as a successful CEO/entrepreneur would make her a formidable opponent and possibly even the frontrunner in the matchup.

The *New York Times* once listed Whitman among the women most likely to be elected the first female president of the United States. At the time of entering the campaign, Whitman was the CEO of eBay with a personal net worth of $1.3 billion, making her the fifth-wealthiest woman in the state. As the darling of Silicon

Valley and the Republican Party, many expected her to raise and spend an unprecedented amount in order to win the gubernatorial race. Expectations were met and exceeded. When all was said and done, Whitman had spent $144 million of her own money and $178.5 million in total. At the time, this was the most spent by a self-funded candidate in U.S. history. In comparison, Brown spent roughly $36 million and prevailed.

But he had help.

The governor's office is vitally important to California's labor unions. The governor has the ability to sign laws, implement regulations, and propose state spending, all of which has a tremendous amount of impact on the state's working families. Ceding the governorship to a Republican businessperson would pose a tremendous threat to funding for public school teachers and health and safety workers and policies that protect worker wages and workplace safety. Keeping a Democrat in the executive office of the state was labor's top political priority.

The threat was real. Republican celebrity Arnold Schwarzenegger replaced recalled Democratic Governor Gray Davis in 2003 and went to war with organized labor. As governor, Schwarzenegger qualified ballot initiatives in 2008 that would curtail state funding for essential safety net services and eviscerate the ability of labor unions to participate politically. The state's labor unions mobilized a massive statewide campaign that successfully defeated the governor's ballot measure package, but it was clear that they did not want to have to do it again with a new Republican governor who was considered a Schwarzenegger clone.

In order to determine the best strategy for defeating Whitman with their limited campaign resources, the labor unions conducted extensive polling on California's swing voters, hoping to find the Kryptonite that would allow them to level the playing field against their billionaire foe. The research identified 2.8 million persuadable swing voters that could be the margin of victory for Brown. What was astonishing was that Asian Americans were more than twice as likely to be among these voters.

Getting these targeted voters to vote for Brown became the Million More Voters (MMV) independent expenditure program. Reaching and turning out swing Asian American voters became the top priority, and I was brought on to advise the program's effort to persuade Asian American voters to support Brown in the general election runoff against Whitman. Notably, three of the top leaders in the California labor movement driving the effort to elect Brown were Asian Americans. Angie Wei was the executive director of the California Labor Federation AFL-CIO, Dave Low was the executive director of the California School Employees Association (CSEA), and Courtni Pugh was the executive director of Service Employees International Union (SEIU) California State Council. All three are known as hardball political players that play to win and this would not be a half-assed check-the-box effort.

Words do not exist to adequately describe the level of skill, tenacity, and resources these three could bring to bear or the historic nature of their accomplishments and position in organized labor. These three strongly supported the effort to target Asian American voters and for me to be a part of consulting team. Typically, Asian Americans in high positions shy away from hiring other Asian Americans for fear of how people would perceive it.

There are three things you need to know about Angie, Dave, and Courtni. One, anyone who knows them knows that they can hold their own in any space and give zero fucks what anyone thinks. Two, absolutely no one is better at their jobs than Angie, Dave, and Courtni. Three, they don't tolerate any level of incompetence and would not have recommended me just to be a token on the campaign. There just was too much riding on winning this race. I couldn't fuck this up because it might be the only chance for us to prove to the political establishment that Asian American voters could be the margin of victory for Democrats in tough races.

Doug Herman at the Strategy Group was the general consultant for the overall effort. I would work with him on the Asian American piece along with Clark Lee, who handled the statewide field outreach effort involving Asian language phone banks, automated calls, and canvassing. Legendary pollster David Binder conducted the voter opinion research.

The first task was to develop a research instrument (poll) to be conducted in the top three Asian languages (Mandarin/Cantonese, Korean, and Vietnamese) that would accurately assess what issues and endorsements would motivate these swing Asian American voters to support Brown. From past experience, I knew that it was pointless to test the persuasive power of Asian American elected officials, civil rights organizations, and celebrities. We've polled them a million times for candidates and ballot measures and the data always came back showing that they had very little impact on how Asian Americans voted. Polling costs a lot of money and the more questions you ask, the more it costs and more likely that the respondent fails to complete the entire survey. I proposed a radical departure from past practice. I suggested that we poll what I called "iconic validators." These weren't specific people. Instead we would poll generic titles of professions venerated in Asian American culture like "educator," "police officer," "doctor," and "business leader."

The polling came back and validated my hypothesis that the endorsement of these "iconic validators" would have more impact on persuading Asian American voters to support Brown than actual Asian American elected officials, organizations, or celebrities. Armed with that knowledge, I set about to assemble a Noah's Ark of Asian American validators in key iconic professions. I was able to secure a diverse group of 15 validators comprised of a doctor, teacher, business leader, faith leader, and first responder in each major ethnic group

(Chinese, Korean, and Vietnamese) in less than two weeks that would be willing to appear in MMV's AAPI mailers and digital ads. I also organized an additional group of Asian American business leaders and education leaders for use on the MMV AAPI website and for the earned media program. This included securing usable images and approvals for quotes from these endorsers under incredibly short deadlines.

Mail pieces were developed based on the topics that polled the strongest with Asian American voters. The copy was initially written in English and then translated by a professional 24-hour service into Chinese (Mandarin and Cantonese are spoken variations, but written Chinese is basically universal), Korean, and Vietnamese. Once the initial translations were completed, I sent them to a volunteer group of bilingual Chinese, Korean, and Vietnamese with experience in political campaigns that I organized to review translated copy for message and direct translation accuracy. Once the copy was approved, the design house was given the translated text to cut and paste into the mailers.

The semi-final mailers were reviewed once more by the volunteer group to ensure that the graphic designer had pasted the translated copy correctly. In several instances, significant cut-and-paste errors were caught and corrected. In one mail piece the line "Meg Whitman did not bother to vote in 28 years" was incorrectly translated to "Meg Whitman did not mind voting for 28 years." This was a major translation mistake that was quickly identified and rectified by our checks and balances system within less than 24 hours. I also provided specific feedback on images used in ads, the website, and mailers and made recommendations to authentically represent AAPI sub-ethnic groups targeted by MMV. In contrast, Whitman's campaign was criticized for damaging cultural gaffes like using distinctively Hmong images in their Vietnamese and Korean language mailers.

No stone was left unturned to reach Asian American voters. Earned media was an important avenue to communicate to Asian Americans, and the MMV program included AAPI press conferences, regular press releases to AAPI press outlets, and an op-ed effort promoting the MMV effort and the Brown candidacy to AAPI press. We worked with Asian media outlets and produced major stories regarding the MMV program and the outreach to AAPI voters. Korean and Chinese print and online media covered the story. In fact, the effort yielded an exclusive two-day story in the *Chinese Daily News*—the largest Chinese daily paper in California. I was also responsible for monitoring online ads to ensure proper execution of the placement strategy and alerted MMV when English language ads were running on Chinese language sites.

Another innovation we introduced to the campaign was a standalone Asian American landing page for the MMV campaign. The original approach was to direct Asian Americans to the main website and they would have to look for the Asian American tab. This would have made it more difficult for Asian Americans to find salient information and key points about Brown's record. Instead, the mailers and digital ads provided links to the Asian American landing page that had prominent buttons that would send visitors to pages with information in their language of choice.

To supplement Clark Lee's live Asian language voter contact program, I organized a group of bilingual Chinese (Cantonese and Mandarin), Korean, and Vietnamese speakers in the span of 48 hours to record three sets of automated in-language GOTV calls.

The Million More Voters campaign was an independent expenditure program that was not subject to campaign expenditure limits. As such, we were prohibited by law from communicating and coordinating our efforts with Brown's campaign. Brown's campaign did have its own AAPI program and was advised by Maeley Tom.

Ultimately, Asian Americans who voted for Arnold Schwarzenegger 62% to 37% in 2006 switched support 55% to 38% for Brown over Whitman—a 42-point swing. This validated the Million More Voters campaign's approach to reaching AAPI voters and showed the state's political establishment that AAPI voters could indeed dictate the outcome of big elections.

Shark Fin Ban

"We don't see things as they are, we see them as we are."

—ANAÏS NIN

In 2011, conservation organizations and animal welfare advocates proposed California legislation to ban the import, sale, and distribution of shark fin in California. The bill, AB 376, was designed to eliminate California as a market for shark fins and thereby reduce the global consumption of shark fin that threatens the existence of the iconic apex species. At the time, 73-90 million sharks per year were being killed globally for their fins and California was the largest market for shark fin in the United States.

When I was approached to consult on this bill, I had my doubts. The science was sound, but the issue was volatile. Handled poorly, the effort would have a tremendous negative impact on the Asian American community far beyond just those who traded or served it. I grew up eating shark fin soup at family association banquets and weddings. I knew the cultural significance of it and the economic impact it would have on segments of the community. Shark fin is almost exclusively consumed by Chinese, and the proposal could have easily been characterized as a racist attack at worst and culturally insensitive at best. The bill also posed a legitimate threat to California's multimillion-dollar shark fin industry.

But as a Chinese American, I also had a strong cultural commitment to the preservation of the environment. Harmony with nature is a prominent theme in Chinese philosophy and religion. I also bristled at the implication that the totality of the cultural identity of Chinese Americans would be reduced to a single soup dish. Many years later I was reminded of this resentment when Tony Leung's Wen Wu character in Marvel's *Shang-Chi* lamented that he, as one of the most powerful and feared individuals on earth, would be named after a chicken dish by the westerner who misappropriated his identity.

> "He appropriated Ten Rings, my Ten Rings, but because he didn't know my real name… do you know what name he chose? The Mandarin. He gave his figurehead the name of a chicken dish." —Wen Wu, Marvel's *Shang-Chi*

I wasn't about to be defined by a fish dish, so I decided to take on the contract at one-fifth of my standard fee on two conditions. First, the bill had to be authored by a Chinese American legislator. Second, Chinese American voters would be polled on the issue and Asian Americans would be at the forefront of the campaign instead of the predominantly white faces of the environmental movement. The sponsors agreed and I went to work. I devised a complete Asian-based wraparound grassroots multi-media campaign and messaging strategy to blunt anticipated opposition arguments that AB 376 discriminated against Chinese Americans.

Assemblymember Paul Fong courageously agreed to carry the bill, AB 376. He was a visionary leader in the AAPI empowerment movement and an ardent environmentalist, and he represented a district with a heavy Chinese American population. The AAPI community in Silicon Valley referred to him as the godfather of Asian American politics. As political director for the Asian American Small Business PAC, I coordinated the independent expenditure campaign that helped elect him in a contentious race for the Assembly in 2008.

We both knew that this would be a fight that could end his political career. But he had faith in Asian American voters and believed that they had more complex political concerns than the preservation of a popular and venerable soup dish.

According to polling the sponsors conducted in English *and* Chinese, he was right. A super-majority of Chinese Americans supported the ban on the sale of shark fins based on the impact of finning on the environment and concerns about the sustainability of the ocean apex species.

The poll, commissioned by the Monterey Bay Aquarium, was conducted by the public opinion survey firm Fairbank, Maslin, Maullin, Metz & Associates. The survey of 600 registered voters found that 76% of all voters and 70% of the oversampled Chinese Americans surveyed supported AB 376. Notably, 69% of those who had eaten shark fin soup expressed support for the proposed legislation, including 65% of California Chinese American voters. The survey results for Chinese Americans were consistent with an online reader poll conducted by the *World Journal*, a daily Chinese language newspaper serving overseas Chinese and Chinese Americans in North America. In that poll, 67% of respondents favored a ban on the shark fin trade, 20% were opposed, and 13% had no opinion.

The aquarium-commissioned survey was also consistent with the growing opposition to shark finning in China itself. A 1,000-person survey conducted in 2009-2010 by the University of Hong Kong Social Sciences Research Center for BLOOM, an international ocean conservation organization, found that 85% of Hong Kong consumers strongly or moderately supported a ban on the import of shark fins to Hong Kong, and 78% accepted having no shark fin soup at wedding banquets.

As expected, vocal opposition to AB 376 came from influential Chinese merchants in San Francisco, Oakland, and Los Angeles. Opponents of AB 376 organized large groups of Chinese Americans to testify against AB 376 in committee and to meet with key legislators prior to floor votes in each house. In addition, opponents mounted an aggressive earned media campaign in the Chinese press, broadcast television, and radio denouncing AB 376 as an attempt to deny Chinese Americans of their civil rights. We heard rumors that the opponents of AB 376 also hired two top-tier lobbying firms and former Assembly Speaker Willie Brown to kill AB 376.

AB 376 needed a formal AAPI voice to deliver the message that the ban on shark fin was not discriminatory. The co-sponsors of the bill—Monterey Bay Aquarium, WildAid, Oceana, and the Humane Society of the United States—used their reach to recruit NBA star Yao Ming and a clutch of celebrity Asian American chefs to voice their support for the ban and demonstrate ways to replicate the soup without using actual shark fin.

To reinforce this effort, I organized the Asian Pacific American Ocean Harmony Alliance (APAOHA - rhymes with "Aloha") to serve as the AAPI voice in support of AB 376. We boldly kicked off the effort to pass AB 376 in the heart of the California shark fin industry, San Francisco, on Valentine's Day 2011. The announcement was made at the California Academy of Sciences in Golden Gate Park and featured Assemblymember Fong; the co-chairs of APAOHA, James Lau (the former policy director of the California League of Environmental Voters) and Judy Ki (a retired Chinese American science teacher); and celebrity chef Charles Phan (founder of the Slanted Door in San Francisco). Across town, state senator Leland Yee ran a counter-press event with Chinese restaurant owners and ate shark fin soup for the television cameras to protest the impact AB 376 would have on Chinese business and culture.

To ensure message discipline and enhance the credibility of the effort, I crafted authentic and persuasive Asian arguments and message points to support AB 376 and helped recruit key AAPI influencers to join APAOHA, including: actress Kelly Hu, Hong

Kong celebrity Sharon Kwok, author Maxine Hong Kingston, San Francisco Assessor Phil Ting, and San Francisco President of the Board of Supervisors David Chiu. I constructed a website and Facebook page for APAOHA with English and Chinese language content supporting AB 376 and launched a Change.org petition that garnered 27,000 signatures. All of these efforts were backed up by a small army of AAPI entrepreneurs, environmental activists, and scientists like Sue Chen, Rebecca Lee, Yvonne Chu, Chris Chin, Claudia Li, Kevin Huang, Ling Ling Yeh, Andrea Gung, Cherilyn Jose, and Michael Kwan. We even recruited renowned AAPI civil rights lawyers to pen a letter dismissing the allegation that the AB 376 shark fin ban was discriminatory.

Hawaii was the first state to ban shark fin, but the effort in California drew global media attention. Moreover, grassroots Asian environmental activists in the United States, Canada, and Hong Kong weighed in on social media in support of the bill. Sharon Kwok, a well-known actress and philanthropist from San Francisco living in Hong Kong, was particularly effective as a spokesperson in support of AB 376 with the Chinese-language media.

The opponents of AB 376 organized busloads of Chinatown residents to make the trek to Sacramento to testify against the bill. We countered with our own Asian Americans who traveled to Sacramento to voice their support for the ban. While our numbers were somewhat less than the opposition's, they effectively demonstrated that the Asian American community was split on the issue and prevented the opponents from effectively painting the proposal as anti-Asian.

To further reduce the blow to Asian American businesses, the sponsors of the bill built in an extended implementation date that would allow these businesses to disgorge their shark fin stock with limited loss in profit and adapt to the trade restriction. Fong also made sure the bill included provisions to provide additional state support and education to the Chinese American community in order to facilitate their good faith cooperation and compliance with the law.

Throughout the course of the campaign it was a struggle to keep AAPIs at the forefront of the effort. We had to push back on well-meaning environmentalists who went off message on several occasions and at times questioned our strategy. A tremendous amount of credit goes to the tireless efforts of Jennifer Fearing (representing HSUS and Oceana), Mike Sutton (representing the Monterey Bay Aquarium), and Peter Knights (representing WildAid) for managing the environmental partners and faithfully supporting the decision to make Asian Americans the vanguard voice of the campaign. Their sensitivity and respect for the Asian Americans on both sides of the debate was truly admirable.

The most frustrating aspect of this campaign was the consistency with which mainstream journalists downplayed the significant AAPI support for the ban and focused heavily on the stereotypical opposition talking points coming from the Chinese American business community. Ironically, the Chinese language newspapers were far better at balanced coverage of Asian American support and opposition for the bill.

Nevertheless, our unconventional grassroots organizing effort and earned media strategy did enough to diffuse the opposition's messaging and organizing efforts. Despite spirited opposition from four AAPI legislators, the effort convinced the remaining seven AAPI legislators to break rank and vote in support of AB 376. Ultimately, the effort to create a pro-ban AAPI narrative played a pivotal role in convincing the Legislature to send AB 376 to Governor Jerry Brown's desk for signature.

Once it was on Governor Brown's desk, we knew that the toughest part of the fight was ahead of us. The dominance of progressive Democrats in the legislature along with a handful of conservationist Republicans almost assured passage in the state Assembly and Senate.

Despite the efforts of two of the most powerful lobbying firms in Sacramento, advocates for the ban held and leveraged the moral high ground against the weaker arguments of the opposition.

Getting a signature from Governor Brown was an entirely different proposition. Brown was a staunch environmentalist, but more focused on climate and clean energy than wildlife conservation. He also served as mayor of Oakland, home to a robust Chinatown with many businesses selling shark fins that were vocally opposed to AB 376. While we worked diligently to diffuse the impression that the bill was anti-Chinese, it was not lost on us that Brown defeated Republican Meg Whitman in 2010 for the governorship with the help of AAPI swing voters. Understandably, this bill was a messy political situation that a sitting governor would rather not have to weigh in on.

We also worried that this very narrow bill would get lost under the mountainous pile of other policy proposals with broader impact and greater urgency under consideration by the governor. The ecological collapse caused by shark finning was at its worst decades away. The governor would have good reason to reject the proposal and give opponents and supporters more time to work out a compromise. The lack of urgency and the crush of competing issues seeking the governor's approval before the constitutional deadline to sign or veto bills on his desk were our biggest stumbling blocks.

Jennifer Fearing was concerned that this phase of the effort would be the most difficult. While some of the pro-ban advocates urged restraint in lobbying the governor, Fearing advocated for an aggressive publicity campaign to keep this issue at the top of everyone's mind until it got signed into law. Fearing is one of the most effective and relentless public interest advocates outside of organized labor to walk the halls of the Capitol. Her ability to wield moral authority and clear and concise arguments through social media channels more than compensates for her lack of political action committee resources.

By this time in the process, most of my work was done. I had established a credible and durable narrative that a significant segment of Asian Americans and Asians around the world supported California's proposal to ban shark fin trading and that the proposal was not anti-Chinese. While Paul Fong had lost some supporters as a result of carrying the bill, he also won over new supporters as the intrepid author of this landmark wildlife conservation legislation. Each side's effort to organize for and against the bill challenged and transformed public and political perception of AAPIs. The fight was intense and at times it got personal. But again, I thought to myself that if I was going to pick a side, it's better to win.

In the final days before the signing deadline, Fearing proposed what we would later come to affectionately call "stunt advocacy." Our goal was to execute as many whacky publicity stunts as possible for the remainder of time left before the signing deadline in order to keep the issue from being buried by other issues. She reasoned that continued press attention would make it harder for the well-heeled opponents to quietly kill the bill behind closed doors as the media pursued other issues on the governor's desk. This led to some insanely fun and outrageous hijinks.

Our first salvo was to construct and attach large foam board fins to cars and trucks and circle the convoy around the Capitol. We called the convoy "the AB 376 jawgernaut." Admittedly, we had a few unfortunate "fin-cidents" during staging (the fins kept falling over), but we persevered and circled the Capitol several times, honking annoyingly as the media videotaped our antics. In addition to garnering local news media coverage (and making total fools of ourselves) we uploaded a video of the stunt onto YouTube that received even more coverage by the Capitol's online news sources and was viewed by hundreds of Capitol staff and legislators. Fearing and Knights enlisted celebrities Bo Derek, Leonardo DiCaprio, and billionaire Richard Branson to publicly urge the governor to sign AB

376 through calls and social media posts. The well-known cartoonist Jim Toomey of *Sherman's Lagoon* fame penned a clever and supportive drawing that ran in newspapers across the country.

Our final Hail Mary play was to produce a video borrowing heavily from *Saturday Night Live*'s popular "LandShark" skit. Governor Brown had a hugely popular corgi "first dog" named Sutter, and the premise of the video would be that a school of corgi sharks journeyed to the Capitol to recruit Sutter's support in the effort to save sharks. The video was titled the "Corgi Fintervention" and involved a small army of adorable but unruly corgis (crowd-sourced through a call for corgis on Fearing's Facebook page), some small foam fins, an unfortunate corgi deposit on the doorstep to the Capitol (we scooped it up), and some very amateur video editing.

This last stunt got a lot of online attention and commentary by the Capitol community and definitely kept everyone's attention on this niche issue as the deadline loomed. We got confirmation that the governor's staff—working round the clock to disposition hundreds of bills before the final deadline—shared the video with their colleagues, who agreed the video was charming and evidence of the dogged determination of AB 376 supporters.

I guess we'll never be able to prove that these stunts really had any impact or if the visionary governor just simply decided to do the right thing on the merits of the proposal. (Those who know Governor Brown well probably would say the latter). What we do know is that our authentic and earnest publicity campaign dominated the capital's social media and digital media ecosystem and helped us garner the earned media attention we wanted.

Governor Brown signed the bill into law on the final day of the deadline with this statement:

> "The practice of cutting the fins off of living sharks and dumping them back in the ocean is not only cruel, but it harms the health

of our oceans."

The AB 376 campaign won me a Reed Award from *Campaigns & Elections* magazine.

Two years later in 2012, Assemblymember Paul Fong won re-election to his final term in the Assembly 62% to 38% despite concerns that he would face Asian American voter backlash from carrying the bill to ban the trade and sale of shark fins. AAPI voters were the largest ethnic voting bloc representing 14%, half of which were Chinese American, of the district.

A decade later the United States Congress passed the Shark Fin Sales Elimination Act, which was signed into law by President Biden at the end of December 2022. In a January 2023 article published in the *Santa Cruz Sentinel*, California Department of Fish and Wildlife law enforcement officer Captain Patrick Foy states, "I think it's safe to say that the (California) shark fin ban…has significantly reduced the black market for shark fins."

CHAPTER 9

Sonia Chang-Díaz

"The greatest test of courage on earth is to bear defeat without losing heart."

—ROBERT GREEN INGERSOLL

Sometimes the fights you lose teach you more than the fights you win.

Sonia Chang-Díaz is a former public school teacher and the first Latina and AAPI to serve in the Massachusetts Senate. In 2022 she ran for governor of Massachusetts.

I didn't know Sonia Chang-Díaz when I made the maximum donation allowed by law to her campaign for governor of Massachusetts, but I did know what she represented. She represented a crossroads for AAPIs all across the country. A choice. An opportunity to show the nation who we are and what we are made of. A test of character, if you will.

Was it because she was favored to win? No. She was a scrappy long shot against a well-funded, well-accomplished candidate who was supported by the state's political establishment. This moment for AAPIs was not about whether she would win or not. This moment was about how we face adversity and whether we see ourselves as individuals or as a community. It's easy to side with a sure bet. It's hard to stand with the long-shot outsider.

I know. I've seen this movie many times before. I had just ended a trailblazing 30-year career running multimillion-dollar campaigns and successfully electing numerous AAPIs to local, state, and federal seats. Many of these AAPIs were dark horse candidates in highly competitive races. You would think the hardest, most soul-crushing part of the job was when the Establishment told these AAPI candidates that they couldn't win or didn't have "the right stuff" to serve.

Well, you would be wrong.

The hardest, most soul-crushing part of the job was when prominent AAPIs told us that we couldn't win and that's why they wouldn't support us. They would say things like, "She should wait her turn" or "she's lost too many times before" or "I like him but he just doesn't look like a governor" to justify why they weren't hosting a fundraising event, making a max contribution, or asking their friends to donate.

John Chiang, California's state treasurer and former state controller, ran for governor and despite his best efforts he could not get America's Asian community and the trillions in net wealth they controlled to sufficiently fund a victorious campaign. While many AAPIs did donate significant sums of money to support Chiang, the overall support did not come close to meeting the full political spending potential of America's wealthy AAPI population. The message that the Establishment heard was that Asian Americans would rather spend their millions on luxury purchases than to back one of the most qualified and experienced candidates to run for governor in the state with most Asian American voters in the nation. They chose status over power. They chose comfort over courage. Merit wasn't even in the equation.

Most of these prominent AAPIs got to where they were by towing the line and by currying favor with the Establishment. Careers were spent chasing invites to White House receptions, getting selfies with prominent officials and celebrities, collecting honorific but powerless titles, and picking political winners that would appoint them to ever higher and more prominent positions in the halls of power. They wanted the access and influence that was much easier to acquire by acquiescing to those already in power. How they all got to where they were guaranteed that they would be averse to risking status for the price of principle. It's human nature. It's survival. It's being the most favored house boy on the political plantation.

However, if we don't start making a different decision moving forward, we will never solve the dilemma of why we have been so powerless and ineffective at stopping the politically instigated epidemic of anti-AAPI hate that has terrorized our communities. It's easy to tweet or TikTok some performative declaration of solidarity and outrage or reduce the work of equity and justice to the simple need to share our stories. It's much harder to sacrifice status by openly spending or raising money in support of an AAPI candidate that the Establishment doesn't want to give a seat at the table to.

Representative Shirley Chisholm was the first Black woman elected to the United States Congress. She once said, "If they don't give you a seat at the table, bring a folding chair." I don't believe the quote is entirely accurate. She didn't bring a folding chair; she took a seat that was already there. There are only so many seats at the table. That's why they are so important and powerful. With all due respect and admiration to Representative Chisholm, I would add this corollary: A seat at the table is not given; it is taken.

Taking a seat that "belongs" to someone else isn't easy. It isn't a spelling contest or a footrace. It's a dog fight. It's messy. You'll make enemies, but you'll also make friends. Win or lose, these fights and how you fight them define you and those around you.

Shortly after outperforming expectations by garnering nearly 30% of Massachusetts Democratic delegates at the state convention and becoming the first woman of color to qualify for the governor's ballot in Massachusetts, Sonia courageously sent out this difficult email to supporters:

> "...a good leader calls the question and focuses resources not just on themselves — but on the best way to build our power

and win real change for the long-term. I've never shied away from being honest — even when it was hard. And that's why I'm being honest with you today. I have looked at the variables from every direction and, unfortunately, there is no path I can, in good faith, lead my supporters on that results in me becoming governor this year."

So instead of leading supporters on a path that would needlessly consume their precious hopes, time, and money, Sonia "took one for the team" and stepped aside to ease Massachusetts Attorney General Maura Healey's historic effort to flip the Massachusetts governor's office from red to blue and become the first out gay and first woman to be elected governor of the Bay State.

Sonia Chang-Díaz's decision was hard. Very hard. Losing is never fun or easy. More importantly, even though she lost, she isn't a loser. She ran an enchantingly admirable campaign, inspiring many, and bringing important issues and ideas to the debate that otherwise wouldn't see the light of day. She is an Asian and Latina face that young people of color could see and say "maybe I can run for governor too." She made me proud to be an AAPI, and her honest and fearless candidacy inspired me at a time when I thought I had lost faith.

Make no mistake, there were losers and those losers were us. What I know from the race is that we as AAPIs could have done more. Not necessarily to just win this race, but to find in ourselves the character to stand steadfastly by her side and help give her a fair shot as she mounted this improbable challenge against the odds.

This was our opportunity to say to the nation and each other that, win or lose, no AAPI will ever be alone whether it is when walking down a street or when endeavoring for a seat at the table where the big decisions are made.

(Note: This is a modified version of an opinion piece I posted on medium.com and thetablenews.com.)

CHAPTER 10

Everyone Was "Kung Flu" Fighting

"Only in the darkness can you see the stars."

—MARTIN LUTHER KING, JR.

Following several painful and disturbing years of Trump and MAGA-fueled anti-Asian racism, Asian Americans reflexively delivered huge gains for the Democratic Party. In addition to delivering the margin of victory to Democrats in key congressional races and reducing what was anticipated to be a red wave in 2022 into a red whimper, Asian American Democrats won election to a historic number of local, state, and federal seats from coast to coast.

In California, voter data vendor Political Data, Inc. reported that Asian American voters consistently outperformed other ethnic groups in turnout as a percent of their number of registered voters. These votes contributed to Representative Katie Porter's successful re-election in a year when she was highly vulnerable to defeat. According to the AAPI Civic Engagement Fund, the significant bloc of Asian American voters in Porter's district favored her 53% to 36%. The poll found that Asian Americans nationally favored Democrats over Republicans 51% to 37%. The *Washington Post* reported an APVote Cast poll that showed Asian Americans favored Democrats 64% to 34%.

Similarly, the Asian American Legal Defense and Education Fund (AALDEF) conducted exit polls that showed Asian American voters favored Democrats 69.6% to 25.6% in the Nevada U.S. Senate race and 74.4% to 21.8% in the Pennsylvania U.S. Senate race, which suggests that the AAPI vote was the margin of victory for Democrats Catherine Cortez Masto and John Fetterman and thereby helped the Democratic Party to retain control of the United States Senate.

In Georgia, national exit polls and reports from several AAPI organizations touted the emergent impact of progressive AAPI voters as the "margin of victory" for Democrat U.S. Senator Raphael Warnock over Republican candidate Herschel Walker.

A poll conducted by the AALDEF found that 78% of AAPI voters supported Democratic Senator Raphael Warnock compared to 22% that favored Republican opponent Herschel Walker. Polling was conducted at five key sites for Asian American voters in DeKalb, Fulton, and Gwinnett counties in the Atlanta metropolitan area. Voters were surveyed in English, as well as four Asian languages: Bengali, Chinese, Korean, and Vietnamese. Warnock beat Walker 51.4% to 48.6% according to the Georgia Secretary of State website.

In a press release, the Asian American Advocacy Fund touted an unprecedented AAPI voter contact program in Georgia that included:

- 152,271 doors knocked
- Over 1.3 million phone calls made to voters
- 167,236 text messages sent to voters
- Over 2 million mailers to AAPI voter households
- Over 1,900 attendees at AAAF events
- 2,202,740 pieces of mail sent
- Digital ad buys across multiple platforms, including Google, YouTube, FB/IG, WeChat, and other ethnic websites, yielding over 34 million digital impressions

- Ethnic media ad buys across 34 ethnic media outlets, yielding over 2.5 million impressions
- Hosted 69 visibility events and 32 hotspot events to directly engage potential voters and provide education on voting

ASPIRE PAC, the political arm of Congressional AAPI Democrats, also issued a press release stating "that its investments in the Georgia AAPI community included: in-language radio ads in Chinese, Vietnamese, and Korean playing throughout Georgia; a paid canvassing operation targeting AAPI voters and Asian businesses that they patronized in Dekalb, Fulton, and Gwinnett counties; in-language literature in five languages dropped at over 8,000 doors; and ethnic media outreach, including television, radio, and print."

In addition, ASPIRE members traveled to Georgia for GOTV weekend, including ASPIRE PAC Chair Grace Meng and Representatives Judy Chu, Pramila Jayapal, Raja Krishnamoorthi, Marilyn Strickland, and Mark Takano. The members attended multiple AAPI canvassing events, AAPI small business roundtables, an AAPI rally, and AAPI houses of worship events.

ASPIRE PAC Chair U.S. Representative Grace Meng issued this statement:

> "Senator Raphael Warnock has demonstrated time and time again that he has the character, competence, and compassion to serve the people of Georgia, including Georgia's growing AAPI community. I'm immensely proud of and grateful for Senator Warnock's efforts to engage Asian Americans in Georgia and how he made language access and AAPI outreach a priority during his campaign. Our AAPI communities in Dekalb, Fulton, and Gwinnett counties were key to his re-election, and that's why ASPIRE also prioritized investments in translated

materials and targeted canvassing to mobilize the Asian American vote. I and ASPIRE have a special relationship with Georgia, and I'm thankful I was able to campaign alongside Senator Warnock this past weekend and see his dedication and commitment to democracy firsthand. Senator Warnock has shown that he will always do the right thing, and work to improve the lives of Georgians, including AAPI Georgians, and I congratulate him on his re-election to the Senate."

Navigator A.M. published results from post-election polling, stating:

"Asian American and Pacific Islander voters tended to vote early during the 2022 midterm elections and remained a strong Democratic constituency. 67 percent of AAPI voters voted by mail or absentee ballot, which is significantly higher than all other racial and ethnic groups, and far higher than the overall electorate (36 percent). AAPI voters leaned Democratic in their partisan identification (57 percent) while backing Democrats at even higher rates: AAPI voters overwhelmingly supported Democratic Senate candidates (net +37; 67 percent Democratic candidates—30 percent Republican candidates) and gubernatorial candidates (net +35; 67 percent Democratic candidates—32 percent Republican candidates), while there was a smaller margin for House candidates (net +28; 62 percent Democratic candidates—34 percent Republican candidates)."

The strong Asian American voter turnout for Democrats also threw a well-deserved karmic wrench into Republican Leader Kevin McCarthy's plan to become speaker of the House of Representatives. Asian American votes allowed the Democratic Congressional Campaign Committee to hold seats in NV-03, CA-09, CA-47, and WA-08 and narrow the Republican House majority enough to allow a small group of rogue Republicans to reject McCarthy's bid for speaker of the House 15 times over the course of five days. McCarthy became the butt of jokes by late night show hosts and precipitated a massive outpouring of memes mocking him on social media. This prompted Indy100.com to describe him as "the most ridiculed man in America."

The role that Asian Americans played in McCarthy's humiliating demonstration of political impotence was delicious payback for his irresponsible use of "China Virus" rhetoric and outlandish opposition to a bipartisan House resolution denouncing hate crimes against AAPIs. McCarthy outrageously claimed, "There is no kitchen in America that thinks this is the priority," as part of his speech in opposition to the passage of the anti-AAPI hate crime resolution.

The only aberration to the AAPI trend in supporting Democrats was in New York where reports indicated that Republican gubernatorial candidate Lee Zeldin carried Chinese American voters in key districts over Democratic Governor Kathy Hochul. Democrats also lost two competitive congressional races in California's heavily Asian American populated Orange County, but reasons are less clear because these races involved Asian against Asian candidates from opposing parties.

While helping Democrats hold control of the U.S. Senate and rejecting a Republican rout of Democrats in the House of Representatives, Asian American Democrats also won a historic number of seats in local, state, and federal races all across the nation.

Hmong American Sheng Thao was elected mayor of Oakland, and Vietnamese American Helen Tran was elected mayor of San Bernardino. Indian American Aruna Miller won election to lieutenant governor of Maryland, and Indian American Shri Thanedar won election to the United States House of Representatives. Rhode Island voters made history and elected Japanese American Linda Ujifusa and Chinese American Victoria Gu to the state Senate. Dr.

Michelle Au, the first Asian American elected to the Georgia state Senate who was redistricted out of the Senate seat, successfully pivoted over to the Georgia House of Representatives.

It's important to understand that these gains did not happen organically or just as a result of demographic growth. The success of Asian Americans this cycle was the product of more and better prepared candidates, a growing engagement among AAPI voters in reaction to anti-Asian sentiment and hate crimes, a growing number of highly skilled career AAPI political operatives holding decision level campaign positions, the work of AAPI activists and advocacy organizations on the ground to convert Asian rage into votes, and an emerging apparatus of AAPI political action funds that are helping to supply critical financial support to Asian American candidates.

The eruption of Asian American Democratic activism in 2022 is clearly the culmination of simmering community resentment that finally bubbled to a boil and resulted in a resounding rebuke of Trump's Republican Party and the epidemic of anti-Asian hate it spawned.

Other Asian American Democratic wins in 2022 included (partial list):

> Tammy Duckworth re-elected to U.S. Senate
>
> Ami Bera re-elected to U.S. House of Representatives
>
> Judy Chu re-elected to U.S. House of Representatives
>
> Pramila Jayapal re-elected to U.S. House of Representatives
>
> Ro Khanna re-elected to U.S. House of Representatives
>
> Andy Kim re-elected to U.S. House of Representatives
>
> Raja Krishnamurthi re-elected to U.S. House of Representatives
>
> Ted Lieu re-elected to U.S. House of Representatives
>
> Doris Matsui re-elected to U.S. House of Representatives

Grace Meng re-elected to U.S. House of Representatives

Bobby Scott re-elected to U.S. House of Representatives

Marilyn Strickland re-elected to U.S. House of Representatives

Mark Takano re-elected to U.S. House of Representatives

Jill Tokuda elected to U.S. House of Representatives

Priya Sundareshan elected to AZ state Senate

Rob Bonta elected to CA state attorney general

Fiona Ma re-elected to CA state treasurer

Aisha Wahab elected to CA state Senate

Dr. Jasmeet Bains elected to CA state Assembly

Mike Fong re-elected to CA state Assembly

Ash Kalra re-elected to CA state Assembly

Alex Lee re-elected to CA state Assembly

Evan Low re-elected to CA state Assembly

Al Muratsuchi re-elected to CA state Assembly

Stephanie Nguyen elected to CA state Assembly

Phil Ting re-elected to CA state Assembly

Nabilah Islam re-elected to GA state Senate

Farooq Mughal elected to GA state House of Representatives

Megan Srinivas elected to IA state House of Representatives

Ram Villivallam re-elected to IL state Senate

Sharon Chung elected to IL state House of Representatives

Jennifer Gong-Gershowitz re-elected to IL state House of Representatives

Hoan Huynh elected to IL state House of Representatives

Theresa Mah re-elected to IL state House of Representatives

Nabeela Syed elected to IL state House of Representatives

Kevin Olickal elected to IL state House of Representatives

Abdelnasser Rashid elected to IL state House of Representatives

Janet Yang-Rohr re-elected to IL state House of Representatives

Tram Nguyen re-elected to MA state House of Representatives

Kumar Bharve re-elected to MD state House of Delegates

Dr. Chao Wu elected to MD state House of Delegates

Stephanie Chang re-elected to MI state Senate

Sam Singh elected to MI state Senate
Ranjeev Puri elected to MI state House of Representatives

Foung Hawj re-elected to MN state Senate

Susan Kaying Pha elected to MN state Senate

Tou Xiong elected to MN state Senate

Ethan Cha elected to MN state House of Representatives

Fue Lee re-elected to MN state House of Representatives

Liz Lee elected to MN House of Representatives

Samantha Vang re-elected to MN state House of Representatives

Kaohly Vang Her re-elected to MN state House of Representatives

Jay Xiong re-elected to MN House of Representatives

Ya Liu elected to the NC state House of Representatives

Duy Nguyen elected to NV state Assembly

Rochelle Nguyen re-elected to NV state Assembly

Iwen Chu elected to the NY state Senate

Anita Samani elected to OH state House of Representatives

Cyndi Munson re-elected to OK state House of
Representatives

Daniel Nguyen elected to OR state House of Representatives

Hoa Nguyen elected to OR state House of Representatives

Hai Pham elected to OR state House of Representatives

Khanh Pham elected to OR state House of Representatives

Thuy Tran elected to OR state House of Representatives

Tarik Khan elected to PA state House of Representatives

Salman Bhojani elected to TX state House of Representatives

Suleman Lalani elected to TX state House of Representatives

Karen Kwan re-elected to UT state House of Representatives
(Kwan was subsequently elected to the UT state Senate in a
special election)

Identity and Power

"Mastering others is strength. Mastering yourself is true power."

—LAO TZU

There are probably hundreds of more stories about AAPIs making a difference that weren't included in this book, but many of the stories I'm aware of weren't mine to tell and I'm sure there are many more I'm just not aware of. The point of this book is to start a real and sustained conversation about the power of politics and curate some of the stories that haven't been told about AAPIs in this space.

This book can't empower you. Your power is already in you. It's been there all this time. Now that you know, it's up to you to believe it and seize it.

In 2015, the California Asian Pacific Islander American Legislative Caucus met for dinner to have a discussion about building out a robust political ecosystem that would support sustainable political power and representation for AAPIs. Ron Wong and I hosted the dinner and we were asked by AAPI Legislative Caucus Chairman Das Williams to walk them through how the Black and Latino community built their political machines because we both had worked closely with Black and Latino elected officials.

We gathered in the private dining room at Ella's, Sacramento's premier dinner spot and the capital's gravitational center of political power. The meeting began as usual and like many times before it didn't seem like we were getting anywhere. A lot of those in attendance had ideas and questions but not much will to really lean into it.

Former AAPI Legislative Caucus Chairman and former Assembly Majority Leader Alberto Torrico had joined us for dinner. Sensing the futility and frustration of the moment, he stood up to speak. He was quiet at first. He looked around the table at each member and then he began to speak.

"Do you all remember that time when a Republican member of the legislature got up to speak and said some horrible things about Asian Americans? Do you remember how all the AAPI legislators got up out of their chairs and shut him down and no ever messed with us again after that?"

Some of the members nodded enthusiastically in agreement and approval. You could see glimpses of bravado and pride. Torrico, still intense, paused to let the moment sink in…and then he said:

"That never fucking happened!"

The members sat in stunned silence.

It was as brutal as it was funny. It was classic Torrico. Alberto, Ron, and I still crack up every time we tell this story. Torrico was making the point that Asian Americans have an identity crisis. Too many AAPIs behave as supplicants clawing for agency in someone else's world instead of as members of a united tribe working together to build their own empire.

I once was invited to a lunch at an exclusive private club by an influential white corporate lobbyist. The ambiance was decidedly smug and stuffy as a club situated a block away from the state's seat of power that only began admitting women in the 1990s would be. We sat down to talk about the Asian American Small Business PAC and its mission to elect AAPI candidates. I asked him to support the PAC and he replied, "Why?" He went on to say that he had all the access that he needed and could get an audience with any AAPI member he wanted to. He didn't need the AASB PAC. He didn't need me. And he brought me to the club to tell me that I was irrelevant with all of his exclusive privileged colleagues serving as the backdrop. The grin on his face was so big he looked like Batman's nemesis, the Joker.

I can't be mad. He was right. At that point AAPI-elected officials didn't empower other AAPIs by forcing institutional lobbyists to work through surrogates like the Latino Caucus did. I didn't have much power and we both knew it. So I graciously thanked him for lunch and decided right then and there to myself that I would work to elect a small army of AAPIs into office without his help. I could hear Jadine's voice again in my head. "Better to win." I did elect that small army of Asian Americans and it turns out I didn't need the help of that lobbyist to do it.

We can't expect to lead or be respected if we don't even know who we are and what we stand for. You don't earn power or inherit it from someone else. It's not collected like a certificate or a degree. You have to wade into the scrum to get a piece of power. It's not civilized or simple. At best, people's feelings get hurt. At worst, careers and lives are destroyed. But that's the price of power.

You could say that the price of power is too high and you'd rather live without it. That's fine, but don't fool yourself into thinking you can do much good or defeat evil without power. Power can be used for both good and evil, but without power you can do neither. Without power you would just be a victim or an observer. Moreover, evil people don't care what the price of power is. They're going to pay whatever the cost or do whatever it takes to get it and use it. To be effective in politics, you have to seize power and wield it.

I don't feel like we're there yet. We can be. It's not like it isn't in our blood or our history. Our ancestors conquered the largest contiguous land empire in world history, terrorized the seas, and built civilizations that laid the foundation for the advancement of humankind. The world's modern military elite still study the tactics and strategies conceived by Asian military strategists and martial artists. Somewhere along the line, aggressive western colonial hegemony washed most of that away. I don't think it's all gone. That fire. That defiance. That ambition. That pride. We just need to keep digging until we find it.

There's a great television show called *Warrior* that aired two seasons on Cinemax and is now streaming on HBO Max. It's based on a treatment written by Bruce Lee about a Chinese immigrant martial arts prodigy, Ah Sahm, struggling to survive the Tong Wars and anti-Chinese racism of San Francisco in the 1870s.

In Season 1, Episode 10 titled "If You're Going to Bow, Bow Low," Ah Sahm is feeling sorry for himself after being beaten badly in combat and is at the end of his rope. He's working menial jobs as a coolie and is asking for a day job from a wealthy local Chinese black market businessman, Wang Chao.

Wang tells Ah Sahm about his journey across the Pacific ocean and how he ended up being sold in Cuba as a slave for 11 years. Out of all the slaves, he was the only one that got free. He asks Ah Sahm, "You know why?" Ah Sahm replies, "Why?" Wang says, "Because I know I'm not a fucking slave."

I replay that scene in my head over and over again on the tough days. Days when the number of racial indignities seems infinite. I appreciated the bluntness of Wang's character, and it reminded me of an AAPI woman who is the epitome of political power, Chung Seto.

Chung served as the New York State Democratic Committee executive director from 2001 to 2005, the first Asian American to serve in that capacity. She also served as the vice chair of the Democratic National Committee's APA Leadership Council. In 2002, the Democratic National Committee's Women's Vote Center honored Chung as a rising star in the Democratic Party and her leadership when it presented her with its first ever Eleanor Roosevelt Award.

In 2013, Chung was campaign manager for John C. Liu, the first Asian American candidate for mayor in New York City. In 2009, Chung led the campaign team that helped elect Liu as New York City comptroller, the first Asian American elected to citywide office, and advised Liu when he made history again by being the first Chinese American elected to the state Senate. Chung also served as senior advisor to Congressmember Grace Meng and managed her successful election as vice chair of the DNC.

One year I was invited to a meeting in DC convened by Congressman Mike Honda with about 50 AAPI political leaders and consultants. The meeting began with going around the table and everyone introducing themselves. Participants would rattle off their titles and accomplishments and the meeting really began to drag even before the substantive discussion to plan a political strategy had even started. The introductions were three-quarters in when we got to Chung. When it came to her turn, all she said was "Chung Seto."

I thought that was the coolest thing ever and so refreshing. It was such a power move. It said to everyone in the room that you should already know who Chung Seto is and if you don't that's your problem. I've thought about that day often, especially when I've felt insecure and the pressure to roll out my credentials in a meeting to prove that I belong in the room. I haven't had that feeling in a very long time because of Chung and I'll be forever grateful to her for that teachable moment in DC.

I get that it's hard to be the nail that sticks up. Standing up for yourself or your community is phenomenally difficult and awkward if you haven't had practice doing it or someone hasn't modeled it for you. Maeley, Georgette, Hilda, Judy, Jadine, Lucy, and Chung set the example for me so when it came time to act accordingly I knew exactly what to do.

In 2015, I was invited to a meeting in San Francisco at Orrick, Herrington & Sutcliffe. Orrick is a global legal powerhouse with over $1 billion in annual revenue. The meeting featured John Podesta, who would be making a presentation on Hillary Clinton's presidential campaign. It was an exclusive group of donors and political players. As I was walking in, everyone carried themselves with the air of "you should know who I am." I was a step behind former Congresswoman and former Under Secretary of State for Arms Control and International Security Affairs Ellen Tauscher. Staff was nervously buzzing around ushering these high-powered guests to the conference room, giving the meeting a pronounced weighty feel.

It had taken me three hours to get into the city that day. I was already irritated. But I saw some AAPI friends and felt a little better about this meeting. These were experienced operatives and one elected official. I recognized other non-AAPI elected officials, political operatives, and some donors. I believe I was invited because I donated to the Ready for Hillary PAC at the urging of Alissa Ko, a rising star in national politics who served in the Obama White House. John Podesta is Democratic Party political royalty. He's advised Presidents Clinton and Obama and now advises President Biden. He doesn't just meet with presidents; he makes them.

He began to go through a slide presentation on why Hillary would win the presidency in 2016. The message was that she was going to win and you wanted to be with the winner. Each slide showed her polling strength with key voter constituencies. One slide was all voters, then just women voters, followed by Black voters and Latino voters. And then the presentation ended and he went into his pitch for money.

At that moment my head exploded. The voice inside my head erupted, "WHAT THE FUCK? Where the fuck is the Asian slide? It's fucking 2015, not 1980!"

I sat there with four AAPI colleagues and could count another five or six in the room. They all sat in silence. At that moment, I thought to myself, *Fuck this.* I got up and climbed over two of my colleagues on my way to the aisle to exit the meeting. Podesta was still talking as I got up and left the room.

I was disappointed at the stunned look on the faces of my colleagues. Their eyes were the size of dinner plates. I'm sure I embarrassed the fuck out of them by making a small scene by leaving as Podesta was presenting. I wasn't sorry and I never asked them how the meeting went or talked about the meeting again. I couldn't care less. The campaign already told me everything I needed to know. I'm sure it didn't mean anything to the Clinton campaign or John Podesta that I left, but I sure as shit wasn't going sit there like some neutered house pet licking myself where my balls used to be.

It's easy to forget who you are and how much power you have. Sometimes we fool ourselves into thinking that status is the same as power. It is not. Status is conferred; power is acquired. Status is celebrated; power is respected. Status is being invited to the meeting; power is the audacity to walk out.

Several years ago, I was hired by a national trade organization to come up with a strategy to kill a bill being considered by the California State Legislature. The author of the bill was the chairman of a powerful Assembly policy committee. The sponsor of his bill was represented by one of Sacramento's perennial top-ten firms and the lead lobbyist was the millionaire managing partner of the firm.

In the process of assessing the situation, I made the mistake of attending the bill's first hearing. After so many years as an invisible Asian American in the halls of the Capitol, I thought no one would notice me sitting in a crowded hearing room that would be considering numerous bills.

I was wrong.

The lobbyist spotted me and stopped in his tracks. He then asked, "What are you doing here?" Half out of curiosity and half out of concern, I replied, "Oh, I'm just monitoring the committee." He didn't buy it and I could see him connecting the dots in his head. It was early in the committee process and there was only one controversial bill on the agenda, and by that time in my career my reputation had finally taken root.

A few hours later I got word from one of California's most powerful politicians "suggesting" that I drop my client.

The point is that you know you have power and relevance when the most powerful people in the state are concerned that you're even in the room.

This is what I want for all Asian Americans. I want us to be the scariest fuckers in the room. I want our competitors and adversaries to be forced to bring their best game when they're up against us. I want allies to need us on the battlefield at their weak side, not on the sidelines as decorative battlements. That's power. That's relevance. But that's on us. We've got to be the best players in the game, stand tall, stand together, do the work, and be prepared to pick a fight.

To be clear, this isn't a call for some kind of twisted AAPI elitism or pseudo-nationalism. Quite the opposite. It is a call for AAPIs to get good enough at the game of politics to meaningfully contribute to the fight for social justice and equity for all oppressed people of color and marginalized communities. Leave your pompoms and bullhorn at home. Bring your sword and shield instead.

In a guest article for the Reappropriate blog, Scott Kurashige recounts civil rights legend Grace Lee Boggs' reflection in her later years on the how she would have approached allyship as an Asian American differently.

Kurashige wrote:

> "Grace also believed it was incumbent on Asian Americans to find our place within the next American revolution. We must, of course, reject model minority assimilationism and its anti-Black connotations. Like Yuri Kochiyama, Grace serves as more than an iconic model of Black-Asian solidarity, but

helps us appreciate how the African American struggle for freedom opened up new possibilities for everyone.

At the same time, she believed it was incumbent on all movement organizers to recognize the distinct perspectives and contributions Asian Americans bring to the revolution. Grace was honored to have been embraced as a member of the Black community and a leader in the Black movement, though she also challenged the erasure of her identity as an Asian American woman. She saw the limitations in any quest for honorary Blackness—a venture that presents problems less pernicious than honorary whiteness but still detracts from the whole humanity of Asian Americans. And if we are not whole ourselves, how can we envision a true revolutionary advance for humanity?"

Kurashige continues:

"Asian Americans have been historically marginalized in—or outright excluded from—many spaces, even among some progressive and left activist organizations. This has created its own barriers towards informed discussion about the place Asian Americans occupy politically. Versions of model minority stereotyping fester even among progressives, who sometimes write-off Asian Americans as naturally passive and hopelessly conservative.

Allyship is essential to movement building. Yet, if Asian Americans are only allowed to see ourselves as allies of others, we risk reducing ourselves to pawns or sidekicks rather than stakeholders. Sidelining Asian Americans within the revolution over-simplifies the realities of racism and undermines possibilities for truly collaborative change.

'I think we've been thinking too much of only workers, white or black, as playing a part in the revolution,' Grace emphasized, as we listened in her living room eight years ago. 'I think it's really time for a change to modify and enlarge our thinking.'"

AAPIs have and can make a huge difference in the trajectory of this nation and in the lives of their fellow people of color. We don't have to be victims or beggars. We have everything we need to define and deliver justice for ourselves and others.

My hope is that this book will inspire you to learn the craft of politics, exercise the courage of leadership that lays dormant inside your DNA, and join the fight to represent the needs and concerns of the powerless.

In other words, you're the hero you've been waiting for. It's time to suit up and get in the game.

Key Takeaways and Campaign Competencies

In Latin, "Si Vis Pacem Para Bellum" translates to "If you want peace, prepare for war." You can't just be willing to get into a fight. You have to train for it. Just like you're not going to be an Olympic champion by reading books about Olympic champions, you're not going to win political fights just by reading political science or history books. Politics is as much an art as it is a science, and the craft needs to be studied as well as practiced.

The key takeaways from this book are:

1. Change requires leadership and the foundation of leadership is character. Leadership is not a mantle or a title; it's a culture. Are you studying the writings and philosophies of great leaders and emulating their actions, or are you simply expecting followers to comply with your demands? Every decision and action you take should reflect and reinforce key qualities of leadership such as humility, trust, empathy, the courage to take on difficult tasks, and the ability to take responsibility for the success and safety of those who you are charged with leading. Some people may think that leadership is about what you can get for yourself, but they would be wrong. Leadership is about what you sacrifice for others.

2. The world will not change without a fight. If you want to change the world, you will have to fight for a seat at the table where decisions are made and resources are allocated. The people currently in the seats will be unwilling to relinquish their place at the table. If a seat is empty, many will vie for it. No one is entitled to the seat. The seat belongs to whoever wins the battle for it. If you want that seat, then you will need to learn and master the skills, strategy, and tactics involved in winning political battles.

3. Once you get a seat at the table, do something with it. It's not enough to hold power. Power must be expended to serve a purpose. Power must also beget more power, so use your seat at the table to bring more people to the table. Politics is a team sport, not an individual endeavor. The team with more players usually wins.

4. Power is status, but status is not power. If you have status, you are only a conduit for someone else's power. Power comes from things that cannot be taken away from you like wisdom, knowledge, skill, decisiveness, patience, discipline, empathy, courage, cunning, and integrity.

5. If you get into a fight or pick a side, it's always better to win.

Here's a list of some of the main skills and competencies you should seek experience in and work to become proficient at if you want to be competitive in the game of politics.

- **Polling.** You should be able to read polling results including cross-tabs. You should know when to conduct a poll, know how to write a poll, understand how to pick a universe for a poll, know how much a credible poll costs, and identify weaknesses or flaws in the polling sample or a poll question. You should also know the difference between quantitative and qualitative research.

- **Messaging Discipline/Crisis Management.** You should know how to fill in a message box, how to draft a crisis communications plan, and how to train a candidate for interviews and debates. The bottom line is to know when to open your mouth and when not to.

- **Cutting Turf.** There are a number of tools and vendors for voter data and you should be proficient at as many of them as you can. It's about defining the pool of voters you plan to communicate with at any given phase of a campaign and being able to use existing vendor tools to generate the lists for use in various voter contact modes (e.g., mail, calls, canvass, text, or digital).

- **Mail.** Mail is still one of the most effective ways to target a voter. Knowing how to maximize your message within the size and shape limits of the mailer is a challenge. Too many words and the reader's eyes glaze over. Too few words and you've missed opportunities to convey key messaging. You should know how mail is designed and produced, how often to send mail, when to send mail, and how to segment your mail. You should also know how to set up a mail tree and track mail.

- **Digital.** Digital encompasses multitudes of platforms, but it is basically any type of paid advertisement (static, video, or animated) that is viewed on a screen…any screen. You need to know about the typical metrics used to measure the efficacy of your digital ad campaign (e.g., impressions, engagement, or acquisition cost).

- **Traditional Broadcast and Cable Media Buying**. For certain races like statewide and national races, purchasing ads on broadcast and cable television is unavoidable. In smaller races, it may not be as cost effective, and in certain expensive media markets it is completely unrealistic. So you have to know where and when it makes sense to buy ads on broadcast and/or cable.

- **Oppo.** "Oppo" is short for opposition research. Most of the time, campaigns hire an opposition research firm to dig into a candidate's financial and personal affairs in order to find weaknesses or flaws that they can attack with campaign ads and mailers. In some cases, it is smart to do defensive "oppo" to determine which flaws your opponents will use against you.

- **Advance.** Advance is a lost political art form. It's about logistics staffing for the candidate/elected official. How to get your candidate from point A to point B in the most effective and efficient way possible and also planning events and appearances that have optimum impact. Things to consider are ease of ingress and exit, planning for security in the event of hostile public interaction, staging an event for the best visual impact, and managing press and media access.

- **Field Management.** Field management involves door-to-door, phone, and text message voter contact. It may also involve relational organizing on social media or through traditional contact modes. Key aspects of this skill are the ability to cut turf, prepare contact lists, manage and organize volunteer and paid contact crews, finding sites to run phone banks or text banks from, and training volunteers and paid contact crews.

- **Fundraising.** Fundraising often holds the highest priority in a race. Without it, nothing else can be done. Fundraising can involve in-person events, Zoom events, direct mail, email, text messages, and direct calls from the candidate to donors. List management, donation page set-up, AB appeal testing, tracking and collecting donations, and donor follow-through are key aspects of campaign fundraising.

- **Compliance.** Compliance refers to both campaign finance compliance and campaign ethics. These rules and standards are complex and change frequently. Campaign operatives and legislative staff should be well-versed and up-to-date on these rules and standards in order to avoid penalties, prosecution, and public relations problems.

The only real and effective way of mastering the competencies is to experience and practice them firsthand in the field. Seek out volunteer positions or take paid campaign positions. Smaller races are usually better places to learn with more opportunities to grow. Bigger races like presidential or congressional races usually have fewer opportunities to learn and grow because they can be very hierarchical and bureaucratic.

Also avail yourself to the various training resources provided by local political party organizations, labor organizations, advocacy groups, and campaign technology platforms. Many campaign technology platforms like Political Data, Inc., ActBlue, and Mobilize have video tutorial pages and blogs.

Historic Timeline of California AAPI State & Federal Officials

1956: Dalip Singh Saund (DEM) elected to the U.S. House of Representatives.

1962: Alfred Song (DEM) and **Mervyn Dymally*** (DEM) elected to the state Assembly.

1966: Alfred Song (DEM) and **Mervyn Dymally*** (DEM) elected to the state Senate. **Wadie Deddeh**** (DEM) and **March Fong Eu** (DEM) elected to the state Assembly.

1968: S.I. Hayakawa (REP) elected to the U.S. Senate.

1972: Paul Bannai (REP) elected to the state Assembly.

1974: Norm Mineta (DEM) elected to the U.S. House of Representatives. **March Fong Eu** (DEM) elected secretary of state. **Mervyn Dymally*** (DEM) elected lieutenant governor.

1975: Floyd Mori (DEM) elected to the state Assembly.

1978: Robert Matsui (DEM) elected to the U.S. House of Representatives.

1980: Mervyn Dymally* (DEM) elected to the U.S. House of Representatives.

1982: Wadie Deddeh** (DEM) elected to the state Senate.

1989: Joyce L. Kennard appointed associate justice to the state Supreme Court.

1991: Matt Fong (REP) appointed to the state Board of Equalization.

1992: Jay Kim (REP) elected to the U.S. House of Representatives. **Nao Takasugi** (REP) elected to the state Assembly.

1994: Matt Fong (REP) elected state treasurer.

1996: Mike Honda (DEM) elected to the state Assembly. Ming Chen appointed associate justice to the state Supreme Court.

1997: John Chiang (DEM) appointed to the state Board of Equalization.

1998: John Chiang (DEM) elected to the state Board of Equalization.

2000: Mike Honda (DEM) elected to the U.S. House of Representatives. **Harry Low** (DEM) appointed state insurance commissioner. **Wilma Chan** (DEM) and **Carol Liu** (DEM) elected to the state Assembly.

2001: Judy Chu (DEM), **Michelle Park Steel** (REP) elected to the state Assembly.

2002: Alan Nakanishi (REP), **Shirley Horton** (REP), **Mervyn Dymally*** (DEM), and **Leland Yee** (DEM) elected to the state Assembly.

2004: Doris Matsui (DEM) elected to the U.S. House of Representatives. **Betty Yee** (DEM) appointed to the state Board of Equalization. **Van Tran** (REP) and **Alberto Torrico** (DEM) elected to the state Assembly.

2005: Ted Lieu (DEM) elected to the state Assembly.

2006: John Chiang (DEM) elected state controller. **Judy Chu** (DEM), **Michelle Park Steel** (REP), and **Betty Yee** (DEM) elected to the state Board of Equalization. **Leland Yee** (DEM) elected to the state Senate. **Kevin De Leon** (DEM), **Mike Eng** (DEM), **Mary Hayashi** (DEM), and **Fiona Ma** (DEM) elected to the state Assembly.

2007: Warren Furutani (DEM) elected to the state Assembly.

2008: Carol Liu (DEM) elected to the state Senate. **Paul Fong** (DEM) and **Mariko Yamada** (DEM) elected to the state Assembly.

2009: Judy Chu (DEM) elected to the U.S. House of Representatives. **Mona Pasquil** (DEM) appointed lieutenant governor.

2010: Kamala Harris (DEM) elected state attorney general. **Kevin De Leon** (DEM) elected to the state Senate. **Dr. Richard Pan** (DEM) and **Das Williams** (DEM) elected to the state Assembly. **Tani Cantil Sakauye** appointed chief justice of the state Supreme

Court.

2011: **Ted Lieu** (DEM) elected to the state Senate. **Goodwin Liu** appointed associate justice of the state Supreme Court.

2012: **Dr. Ami Bera** (DEM) and **Mark Takano** (DEM) elected to the U.S. House of Representatives. **Rob Bonta** (DEM), **Ed Chau** (DEM), **David Chiu** (DEM), **Al Muratsuchi** (DEM), **Adrin Nazarian***** (DEM), and **Phil Ting** (DEM) elected to the state Assembly.

2014: **John Chiang** (DEM) elected state treasurer. **Betty Yee** (DEM) elected to state controller. **Ted Lieu** (DEM) elected to the U.S. House of Representatives. **Kevin De Leon** (DEM) elected president pro tempore of the state Senate. **Janet Nguyen** (REP) and **Richard Pan** (DEM) elected to the state Senate. **Young Kim** (REP), **Kansen Chu** (DEM), and **Evan Low** (DEM) elected to the state Assembly.

2016: **Kamala Harris** (DEM) elected to U.S. Senate. **Ro Khanna** (DEM) elected to the U.S. House of Representatives. **Phillip Chen** (REP), **Vince Fong** (REP), **Ash Kalra** (DEM), and **Al Muratsuchi** (DEM) elected to the state Assembly.

2018: **Fiona Ma** (DEM) elected to state treasurer. **Tyler Diep** (REP) elected to the state Assembly.

2020: **Kamala Harris** (DEM) elected vice president of the United States. **Michelle Park Steel** (REP) and **Young Kim** (REP) elected to the U.S. House of Representatives. **Dave Min** (DEM) elected to the state Senate. **Alex Lee** (DEM) and **Janet Nguyen** (REP) elected to the state Assembly.

2021: Rob Bonta (DEM) appointed attorney general of California.

2022: Rob Bonta (DEM) was elected attorney general of California. **Janet Nguyen** (REP) and **Aisha Wahab** (DEM) elected to the state Senate. **Jasmeet Bains** (DEM), **Mike Fong** (DEM), **Stephanie Nguyen** (DEM), and **Tri Ta** (REP) elected to the state Assembly.

***Mervyn Dymally** was born in Trinidad and of mixed African and Indian descent
****Wadie Deddeh** was of Chaldean descent
*****Adrin Nazarian** is of Armenian descent

During their terms in legislative office, Dymally and Deddeh did not publicly identify as AAPI. Years later, Adrin Nazarian joined the AAPI Legislative Caucus as the definition of AAPI became broader and included individuals who politically self-identified as AAPI. They were included in this list to provide readers with the most comprehensive account of California legislative history. Paul Krekorian (Armenian) preceded Adrin Nazarian in the Assembly in the years 2006-2010 but did not self-identify as AAPI at the time.

Progressive AAPI Political Organizations

Political Action Committees

(Donations are NOT tax deductible as charitable contributions)

ASPIRE PAC

(http://aspirepac.org/)

ASPIRE PAC is the political arm of Asian American and Pacific Islander members of Congress. ASPIRE PAC stands for Asian Americans & Pacific Islanders Rising & Empowering PAC. ASPIRE PAC is focused on supporting candidates of Asian American and Pacific Islander descent and those that support and promote the issues of the AAPI community. ASPIRE PAC offers a voice for the AAPI community and encourages active participation in the U.S. political process. ASPIRE PAC is chaired by Congresswoman Grace Meng, and was launched in 2011 by Congresswoman Judy Chu.

Ronin Project PAC

(https://www.repealtheracism.org/)

The Ronin Project is a 527 political organization that was formed by an elite group of 15 AAPI political consultants in response to the epidemic of anti-Asian hate following Donald Trump's use of "Kung Flu" and "China Virus" during the COVID-19 crisis. The goal of the Ronin Project is to inspire stronger AAPI political participation and execute strategies that exact a high political or economic price from politicians or organizations that choose to weaponize anti-Asian rhetoric and anti-Asian sentiment for political or economic purposes. The Ronin Project is deeply invested in projects and programs that will lay the foundation to support a sustainable progressive AAPI political ecosystem in America.

CAPA21 PAC

(https://capa21.com/)

CAPA21 is an Asian American Pacific Islander political action committee that invests in progressive candidates, AAPI field operations, and projects to improve AAPI participation in the political process. Their vision is of a country where AAPIs have a powerful presence and role in all branches and levels of government and politics, achieved through AAPI voters who are engaged, informed, and empowered. CAPA21 has roots in the Coalition of Asian Pacific Americans, founded in 1988 as one of the country's first AAPI PACs.

Indian American Impact

(https://iaimpact.org)

Impact works to build power for the Indian American and South Asian community and enact progressive change by activating, engaging, and electing Indian Americans and South Asians across the United States, and working with our allies to deliver policies that lift up all communities. Indian Americans are a powerful and crucially important force for progressive change. Impact believes the work of engaging Indian Americans is among the most crucially important work in the country. In 2020, Impact made a bet and invested $15 million in engaging, activating, and mobilizing South Asian Americans, Asian Americans, and Pacific Islanders, especially in Georgia. In the 2020 election, turnout in their communities nearly doubled since 2016 in Georgia, with 30,000 Asian Americans voting for the first time ever. Two-thirds of these voters voted for Democrats, and South Asian Americans made the margin, which was decided by 11,779 votes.

AAPI Victory Fund

(https://aapivictoryfund.com/)

The AAPI Victory Fund—the first Super PAC of its kind—is focused on mobilizing Asian American and Pacific Islander (AAPI) eligible voters and moving them to the ballot box. The AAPI community is joined through their values of hard work, family, and their history as immigrants. With the AAPI eligible voters exceeding that of the margin of victory in numerous districts and states, they have an opportunity under a common agenda to bring AAPI voters into position to make or break outcomes for candidates across the country.

Asian American Action Fund

(https://aaafund.org/)

The Asian American Action Fund is a political action committee that seeks to increase the Asian American and Pacific Islander community's voice in politics at every level of government across the United States.

The AAA-Fund is a progressive political organization that is dedicated to empowering Asian Americans and Pacific Islanders across the United States. Through the AAA-Fund, Asian American Pacific Islanders from different ethnic groups and from all over the country work together to increase the voice of the AAPI community in local, state, and federal government. They do this by helping to elect political candidates who have a demonstrated commitment to the community and by engaging AAPIs in the political process. Since their founding in 2000, they have endorsed more than 200 candidates from every AAPI ethnic community, in every region of the country, and at every level of government. Together, they are building a national network of AAA-Fund chapters, leaders, and activists who are increasing the AAPI community's voice.

501(C)(4) Organizations

(Donations are NOT tax deductible as charitable contributions)

Asian American Power Network

(https://www.aapowernetwork.org/)

AAPN is an alliance of state-based Asian American 501(c)(4) organizations building power to win concrete changes for our local communities and build solidarity across communities of color. They share resources, incubate new organizations through coaching and capacity building, hone best practices and tactics for voter engagement, and implement political strategy to move Asian Americans broadly on progressive policy and racial justice. AAPN is a fiscally sponsored project of the Center for Empowered Politics.

Asian American Advocacy Fund

(https://asianamericanadvocacyfund.org)

The Asian American Advocacy Fund's mission is to advocate for the civil and human rights of Asian Americans, Pacific Islanders, and Native Hawaiians in Georgia. Through a combination of policy advocacy at local, state, and federal levels, and by supporting candidates that believe in their values, they fight to create a better Georgia for all. Their vision is a Georgia where Asian American, Pacific Islander, and Native Hawaiian voices are represented in elected leadership and progressive policies across the state.

Emerging Voters

(https://www.emergingvoters.org/)

Emerging Voters is a 501(c)(4) social welfare nonprofit dedicated to advancing the civic engagement of AAPI voters and promoting the welfare of the AAPI community. Emerging Voters does this by focusing on values important to each of their independent constituent groups, as well as those broadly shared by the AAPI community, and empowering them to become part of organized public life in America. Through values-based and differentiated in-language messaging, Emerging Voters is committed to forging a new path forward around the most pressing policy issues of our time, ensuring that the AAPI community continues to have a place at the table in a representative republic.

AAPI Victory Alliance

(https://aapivictoryalliance.com/)
AAPI Victory Alliance works to build Asian American and Pacific Islander political power across the country by providing education

on progressive issues; creating and advocating for policies that affect our communities; and building alliances with organizations to help AAPIs exert their power and be the margin of victory at the local, state, and national levels. AAPI Victory Alliance will house the first-ever AAPI think tank.

AAPI Power Fund

(https://aapipower.org/)

The National AAPI Power Fund is fiscally sponsored by the Sixteen Thirty Fund, a 501(c)(4) organization that funds lobbying and independent political work. The National AAPI Power Fund (Power Fund) was established in 2020 to support the emerging AAPI voting bloc. They harness the energy, enthusiasm, and potential of this electorate for progressive impact. In the 2020 U.S. presidential and senatorial elections, the Asian American Advocacy Fund (AAAF) led the effort to call 92% of the estimated 238,000 eligible AAPI voters in Georgia. AAAF, with the support of the National AAPI Power Fund, strengthened and expanded Georgia's electorate and also produced a dramatic increase in turnout that ultimately brought Democrats control of the U.S. Senate.

501(C)(3) Organizations

(Donations ARE tax deductible as charitable contributions)

Asian American Women's Political Initiative

(https://www.aawpi.org/)

The Asian American Women's Political Initiative (AAWPI) is the country's only political leadership organization for Asian American and Pacific Islander women. For over a decade, AAWPI's groundbreaking political leadership program for low-income and immigrant AAPI women has been changing the face of political power in Massachusetts. AAWPI's 100+ alumni are Dreamers, anti-foreclosure activists who have experienced foreclosure themselves, LGBTQ rights advocates, and nonprofit entrepreneurs who found their political voice through AAWPI. AAWPI's model addresses the unique challenges AAPI women face, building community around a shared commitment to social justice. Over 90% of AAWPI alumni go on to work on campaigns, become organizers, or run for office themselves. Building on the success of their Massachusetts model for deep, lasting civic engagement, they are scaling nationally and creating a first-of-its-kind national infrastructure to activate AAPI women, elevating civic engagement from voting to community organizing to running for office.

APIAVOTE

(https://apiavote.org/)

Asian and Pacific Islander American Vote (APIAVote) is the nation's leading nonpartisan nonprofit dedicated to engaging, educating, and empowering Asian American and Pacific Islander communities to strengthen their voices and create impact. For 15 years, APIAVote has been at the forefront of a rising movement to ensure AAPIs are represented and heard, leading to historic voter turnout and advancing equity for AAPI communities.

APAICS

(https://www.apaics.org/mission-history)

The Asian Pacific American Institute for Congressional Studies (APAICS) is a national non-partisan, nonprofit 501(c)(3) organization dedicated to promoting Asian Pacific American participation and representation at all levels of the political process, from community service to elected office. APAICS programs focus on developing leadership, building public policy knowledge, and filling the political pipeline for Asian Pacific Americans to pursue public office at the local, state, and federal levels.

CAUSE USA

(https://www.causeusa.org/)

Center for Asian Americans United for Self-Empowerment (CAUSE) is a 501(c)(3) nonprofit, nonpartisan, community-based organization with a mission to advance the political and civic empowerment of the Asian Pacific American community through nonpartisan voter outreach, training, and education as well as leadership development. Founded in 1993, CAUSE is composed of committed professional, business, community, and political leaders, and has established itself as a unique nonpartisan AAPI organization dedicated solely to AAPI civic and political participation.

Recommended Additional Reading

The Art of War by Sun Tzu

Go Rin No Sho: The Book of 5 Rings by Musashi Miyamoto

Spellbound by David Kwong

Fierce and Fearless: Patsy Takemoto Mink, First Woman of Color in Congress by Judy Tzu-Chun Wu and Gwendolyn Mink

Heart of Fire: An Immigrant Daughter's Story by Mazie K. Hirono

I'm Not Who You Think I Am: An Asian American Woman's Political Journey by Maeley Tom

Hardball by Chris Matthews

Words That Work by Dr. Frank Luntz

The Thumpin': How Rahm Emanuel and the Democrats Learned to Be Ruthless and Ended the Republican Revolution by Naftali Bendavid

Buck Up, Suck Up . . . and Come Back When You Foul Up by James Carville and Paul Begala

The Power of Moments by Chip Heath and Dan Heath

Switch by Chip Heath and Dan Heath

Made to Stick by Chip Heath and Dan Heath

The Tipping Point by Malcolm Gladwell

Outliers by Malcolm Gladwell

Blink by Malcolm Gladwell

Rage for Justice by John Jacobs

The Victory Lab: The Secret Science of Winning Campaigns by Sasha Issenberg

Influence: The Psychology of Persuasion by Robert Cialdini

Pre-suasion: A Revolutionary Way to Influence and Persuade by Robert Cialdini

The Fixer: Secrets for Saving Your Reputation in the Age of Viral Media by Michael S. Sitrick

Spec Ops: Case Studies in Special Operations Warfare: Theory and Practice by William H. McRaven

Kamala's Way by Dan Morain

Landmark AAPI Civil Rights Cases

Ho Ah Kow v. Nunan, 12 F. Cas. 252 (C.C.D. Cal. 1879).
The court found San Francisco's "Queue Ordinance" unconstitutional.

In re Ah Chong, 2 F. 733 (C.C.D. Cal 1880).
A U.S. federal court ruled that Chinese residents in California are allowed to fish in California waters.

Tape v. Hurley, 66 Cal. 473 (1885).
The family of Mamie Tape challenged the San Francisco public school system for denying her enrollment in elementary school because of her race. When Tape prevailed in court, San Francisco established a segregated school for Asian American students only.

Yick Wo v. Hopkins, 118 U.S. 356 (1886).
The first case where the U.S. Supreme Court ruled that a law that is race-neutral on its face but administered in a prejudicial manner is a violation of the 14th Amendment's Equal Protection Clause in the U.S. Constitution. This case involved San Francisco's prohibition on laundries operating in wooden structures without a permit. The vast majority of permit applications from Chinese were denied while the vast majority of permit applications from non-Chinese were approved.

United States v. Wong Kim Ark, 169 U.S. 649 (1898).
The U.S. Supreme Court ruled that the Constitution provides anyone born in the United States with birthright citizenship of the United States of America.

Gong Lum v. Rice, 275 U.S. 78 (1927).
The U.S. Supreme Court upheld Mississippi's separate schools system and rules that Asians were not white and therefore allowed to be excluded from white schools. The constitutionality of "separate but equal" schools was upheld by the court in Plessy v. Ferguson, 163 U.S 537 (1896) and later overturned in Brown v. Board of Education, 347 U.S. 483 (1954).

Ozawa v. United States, 260 U.S. 178 (1922).
Ozawa had lived in the U.S. for 20 years and argued that Japanese should be classified as "white" and be allowed to be naturalized under the 1906 Naturalization Act that allowed "free white persons" to be naturalized. The U.S. Supreme Court denied Ozawa naturalization and opined that "white" meant Caucasian. The U.S. Supreme Court doubled down on this approach in United States v. Bhahat Singh Thind, 261 U.S. 204 (1923) when Thind argued that he was eligible for naturalization under the Ozawa decision because he was born as a high-caste Hindu from Punjab, considered by scientific authorities as members of the Caucasian race. The Court rejected Thind's argument and expounded that "free white persons" should only be considered "synonymous with the word 'Caucasian' only as that word is popularly understood."

Korematsu v. United States, 323 U.S. 214 (1944).
Fred Korematsu was arrested and convicted of defying the relocation order for Japanese Americans in WWII. Korematsu challenged the

constitutionality of the order. The U.S. Supreme Court upheld the exclusion of Japanese Americans from the West Coast Military Area during World War II and Korematsu's conviction. The Court argued that the relocation was constitutional based on the military's assertion that Japanese Americans were acting as spies for Japan. Korematsu's conviction was later voided by a California district court in 1983 on the grounds that the United States suppressed a government report that found no evidence that Japanese Americans were acting as spies for Japan.

Oyama v. State of California, 332 U.S. 633 (1948).
The U.S. Supreme Court decided that certain provisions of the 1913 and 1920 California Alien Land Laws abridged the rights and privileges guaranteed by the 14th Amendment in the U.S. Constitution.

Lau v. Nichols, 414 U.S. 563 (1974).
The U.S. Supreme Court ruled that San Francisco's failure to provide different educational programs for non-English speaking Chinese American students was in violation of the Civil Rights Act and led to the national recognition and expansion of bilingual education programs.

Endnotes

Part I: Leaders
Simon Sinek, *Leaders Eat Last* (Portfolio, 2017)

Chapter 1: Character
Paul Davidson, "California Reaches Deal On $15 Minimum Wage," *USA Today*, March 29, 2016

Chapter 2: Vision
Maeley Tom, *I'm Not Who You Think I Am: An Asian American Woman's Political Journey* (2020)

J. Matthews, "Quiet Minority Shifts Tactics In California; Appointee Battle Reflects Asian Americans' Power," *Washington Post*, February 25, 1988

Part II: A Seat at the Table

Chapter 3: Judy Chu, 2001 Assembly Campaign
Rodney Tanaka, "Chu Posts Strong Victory in 49th State Assembly Race," *San Gabriel Valley Tribune*, May 16, 2001

Richard Winton, "Chu Is Known as a Bridge-Builder," *Los Angeles Times*, May 18, 2001

Stephanie Chavez, "Assemblywoman Praised for Reaching Across Ethnic Divide," *Los Angeles Times*, July 1, 2001

Frank del Olmo, "Turning The Ethnic Factor On Its Head," *Los Angeles Times*, May 20, 2001

David Pierson, "Car Dealer, Immigrants Settle Suit," *Los Angeles Times*, April 14, 2014

Nancy Vogel and Carl Ingram, "Pleas Make Crisis Personal," *Los Angeles Times*, February 9, 2003

Christin Bedell, "Speaking Out On Heat Deaths," *Bakersfield Californian*, July 29, 2005

Robert Salladay and Nancy Vogel, "Gov. Orders Shade, Water For Workers Sickened By Heat," *Los Angeles Times*, August 3, 2005

Andrew McIntosh, "California's Tax Amnesty For Tax Shelter Abusers Netted $1.4 Billion—Along With A Big Surprise," *Sacramento Bee*, February 2, 2006

Chapter 4: Judy Chu, 2006 Board of Equalization Campaign

The Battle of Thermopylae: 300 Spartans Against The World, History Cooperative, https://historycooperative.org/the-battle-of-thermopylae-300-spartans-against-the-world/

Chapter 5: Judy Chu, 2009 Congressional Special Campaign

Rebecca Kimitch, "Candidates Crowd Race For 32nd District Seat," *San Gabriel Valley Tribune*, April 13, 2009

"Chu Wins Calif. Demo Party Support Over Cedillo In 32nd CD Battle," *CalPeek Newsletter*, April 2009

Nathan L. Gonzales, "California 32: Race Matters?," *The Rothenberg Report*, April 13, 2009

Part III: The Margin of Victory
Asian American Small Business PAC Campaign Finance Reports, *California Secretary of State*, https://cal-access.sos.ca.gov

Chapter 7: Million More Voters
Mike Royko, "How Jerry Brown Became Governor Moonbeam," *New York Times*, March 6, 2010, https://www.nytimes.com/2010/03/07/weekinreview/07mckinley.html

Kate Zernike, "She Just Might Be President Someday," *New York Times*, May 18, 2008

Mike Rosenberg, Tracey Kaplan, Ken McLaughlin, "GOP Gaffes Were Costly In Effort To Win Asian and Latino Support," *Internal Affairs, San Jose Mercury News*, April 10, 2011

Maeley Tom, *I'm Not Who You Think I Am: An Asian American Woman's Political Journey* (2020)

Chapter 8: Shark Fin Ban
"Sociological Study: Hong Kong Shark Fin Consumption Habits And Attitudes," 2009-10, 2014-15, and 2019-20, https://www.bloomassociation.org/en/bloom-hong-kong/research/

"Paul Fong, 'Godfather' of Silicon Valley's Asian-American political community steps into spotlight," *8Asians.com*, June 8, 2008 https://www.8asians.com/2008/06/08/paul-fong-godfather-of-silicon-valleys-asian-american-political-community-steps-into-spotlight/

Patrick McGreevy, "Brown law signing flurry includes shark fin ban," *Los Angeles Times*, October 8, 2011

Jeremiah Oetting, "California's Ban On Shark Fins Doesn't Stop The Trade From Passing Through Its Ports," *Santa Cruz Sentinel*, January 14, 2023

K. Lapizco, "Biden Signs US Shark Fin Sales Elimination Act," *WorldAnimalNews.com*, December 26, 2022, https://worldanimalnews. com/victory-president-biden-signs-the-shark-fin-sales-elimination-act-helping-to-protect-sharks-in-the-u-s/

Chapter 9: Sonia Chang-Diaz
Sonia Chang-Diaz, email to supporters, June 23, 2022

Chapter 10: Everyone Was "Kung Flu" Fighting
Akemi Tamanaha, "New Poll Finds AAPI Voters May Have Help Dems Over The Line," *AsAmNews.com*, November 9, 2022

"2022 Midterm Voters: Asian Americans and Pacific Islanders," *Navigator*, December 9, 2022, https://navigatorresearch.org/ wp-content/uploads/2022/12/Navigator-Post-Election-Survey-Release-12.09.2022.pdf

Janice Kai Chen, Chris Alcantara, and Emily Guskin, "How different groups voted according to exit polls and AP VoteCast," *Washington Post*, November 8, 2022

Kimmy Yam, "Nevada Is 1 of 5 States With Over 10% Asian Americans. Both Parties Courted Vote, But Dems Won Out," *NBCnews.com*, November 18, 2022

Ross Barkin, "Where Democrats Lost," *Political Currents*, November 10, 2022, https://rossbarkan.substack.com/p/where-democrats-lost

Katherine Fung, "30% of Anti-Asian Incidents in 2020 Used Rhetoric Like 'China Virus,' 'Kung Flu,' Report Says," *Newsweek*, March 18, 2021, https://www.newsweek.com/30-anti-asian-incidents-2020-used-rhetoric-like-china-virus-kung-flu-report-says-1577189

Kimmy Yam, "New Facebook ads tell voters which lawmakers voted against denouncing Asian racism," *NBCnews.com*, October 21, 2020, https://www.nbcnews.com/news/asian-america/new-facebook-ads-tell-voters-which-lawmakers-voted-against-denouncing-n1244058

Barbara Sprunt, Susan Davis, "Kevin McCarthy is elected House speaker after 15 votes and days of negotiations," *NPR*, January 7, 2023

Ariana Baio, "10 Memes That Show Kevin McCarthy Has Become The Most Ridiculed Man In America," *Indie100.com*, January 4, 2023, https://www.indy100.com/politics/kevin-mccarthy-republicans-house-jokes-twitter

Afterword

"Mongol empire," Britannica.com, January 6, 2023, https://www.britannica.com/place/Mongol-empire

Lucy Davidson, "10 Facts About Ching Shih, China's Pirate Queen," HistoryHit.com, November 24, 2021, https://www.historyhit.com/facts-about-ching-shih-chinas-pirate-queen/

Scott Kurashige, "Find your Place in the Revolution: Grace Lee Boggs' Final Message to Asian Americans," *Reappropriate.co*, June 27, 2022, http://reappropriate.co/2022/06/find-your-place-in-the-revolution-grace-lee-boggs-final-message-to-asian-americans/

About the Author

BILL WONG is an award-winning political strategist and author of *Better to Win*. He is a consummate insider whose formidable political knowledge and influence helped shepherd a historic number of Asian Americans into the halls of power.

Bill most recently served as a senior political advisor to California State Assembly Speaker Anthony Rendon. As the political director for the California Assembly Democrats, he managed a $25 million budget per cycle and led efforts that resulted in the largest Assembly Democratic majority in over 130 years. He is now a semi-retired political consultant and offers personalized training and coaching for individuals interested in mastering the craft of political influence.

He has advised Fortune 100 companies, labor organizations, political action committees, nonprofit organizations, and candidates for local, state, and federal office. For ten years, he was the political director for the Asian American Small Business PAC. Bill is also an expert in mobilizing the emergent advocacy, voting, and fundraising power of AAPI communities. He has been included in *Capitol Weekly*'s Top 100 power list from 2018 to 2021.

Bill has over three decades of legislative experience that includes serving as chief of staff to State Assemblymember Anthony Rendon, State Assemblymember Judy Chu, and State Senator Hilda L. Solis, and as legislative director to State Assemblymember Mike Honda. During his tenure in the California State Legislature, Bill successfully developed and guided to passage millions of dollars in state budget funding for essential health and human services programs and groundbreaking legislation on Asian and Pacific Islander issues, wildlife conservation, revenue and taxation policy, and hate crime enforcement.

He earned his Bachelor of Arts degree in Political Science and a minor degree in Asian American Studies at the University of California at Davis and has returned to the university as a guest lecturer. Bill has been a guest on public radio and on Current TV's *War Room* with Jennifer Granholm as a Democratic strategist and expert on AAPI voters. He has been frequently quoted in the *Los Angeles Times*, *Sacramento Bee*, *Politico*, and *CalMatters*.

Bill previously held leadership positions in numerous state and local community organizations and civic commissions, including United States Electoral College (2000) California elector and Sacramento City Planning commissioner. He has received numerous awards for campaigns and community service, including: *Campaigns & Elections* magazine's Reed Award, California Asian Pacific Islander Legislative Caucus Foundation API Heritage Month Award for Public Service, California Asian Pacific Islander Legislative Caucus Award for Leadership, California Democratic Party API Caucus Trailblazer Award, *Asian Enterprise Magazine* Special Advocate of the Year Award, and Asian Pacific Islander Capitol Association Unsung Hero Award.

To learn more or contact Bill, visit www.BettertoWin.com.